STORY DRIVEN

You Don't Need to Compete When You
Know Who You Are

Bernadette Jiwa

'The greatest way to live with honour in this world is to be what we pretend to be.'
—*Socrates*

Published in Australia by Perceptive Press.
www.thestoryoftelling.com

National Library of Australia Publication Data
available via www.nla.gov.au

ISBN: 978-0-9944328-1-0

Printed in the United States of America

Cover Design: Reese Spykerman
Interior Design: Kelly Exeter

10 9 8 7 6 5 4 3 2 1

First Edition

For Adam, Kieran and Matthew—the making of me.
And for Aimee and Leanne.
Your Dad would be so proud of who you are.

CONTENTS

STORY DRIVEN

*You Don't Need to Compete When You
Know Who You Are*

Bernadette Jiwa

PREFACE

'To know who you are is the greatest power of all.'
—Sherrilyn Kenyon and Dianna Love

Every one of us—regardless of where we were born, how we were brought up, how many setbacks we've endured or privileges we've been afforded—has been conditioned to compete to win. Ironically, the people who create fulfilling lives and careers—the ones we respect, admire and try to emulate—choose an alternative path to success. They have a powerful sense of identity. They don't worry about differentiating themselves from the competition or obsess about telling the right story. They tell the real story instead. Successful organisations and the people who create, build and lead them don't feel the need to compete, because they know who they are and they're not afraid to show us. How about you?

What do you stand for?

Where are you headed and why?

What's been the making of you?

What will make your career or company great?

You must be able to answer these questions if you want to build a great company, thriving entrepreneurial venture or fulfilling career. Whether you're an individual or you're representing an organisation or a movement, a city or a country, *Story Driven* gives you a framework to help you consistently articulate, live and lead with your story. This book is about how to stop competing and start succeeding by being who you are, so you can do work you're proud of and create the future you want to see.

WHO ARE YOU—AND WHY DO YOU NEED TO KNOW?

Who are you? In a connected world of less-linear career paths and more opportunities to influence change, this is the big question of our time—the most important question anyone starting a career or a company, and building a life and a legacy, can ask. Our answers can help us to consistently act with integrity and to differentiate ourselves or our organisations by being more, not less, of who we are. But it's a question we have stopped asking in the age of comparison.

Sure, we may have done a bit of personality profiling here and there or had an offsite retreat to work on our branding and external messaging, but these attempts to label ourselves don't often get to the heart of what makes us unique. In a digital world, as the village becomes global, it's never been more important to have a powerful sense of identity and to avoid the temptation of just competing to win.

When I was a kid, and maybe when you were, too, every professional or craftsperson in the village, from the doctor to the baker, knew the particular role he or she played in the community. The people who ran businesses did so with pride. They had a purpose. They were clear about their values and the difference they made. In a globalised world, without the grounding of the village, we don't always have that sense of being visible, contributing members of tight-knit groups or local neighbourhoods. So, in a commercial environment, we have tried instead to understand our competitive advantage. We have become reactive to the competitive landscape, rather than responsive to the needs of our communities—those people we hope to serve. We are so focused on the competition, or even the threat of it, that we've forgotten to double down on what makes us and our work unique and valuable.

It's hard to figure out how to be great at what you do, in the way only you can do it, by focussing on what everyone else is doing. My goal is to give you an alternative—a way to discover (or rediscover) and stay true to who you are and to remain conscious of how your contribution can impact the world.

WE ARE MORE POWERFUL THAN WE THINK

'The most powerful person in the world is the storyteller.'
—Steve Jobs

Stories create change. That's why we've been telling them for generations—to motivate and protect our tribes, to connect and warn each other, to stir hate or spread love. Without stories, we are rudderless.

We like to believe that change happens at the centre, that it begins at the seat of power. We're wrong. All change happens at the edges. It starts with the first person who decides to expose a truth. In doing so, they rewrite the story.

You have an important role to play in shaping tomorrow's world. As an individual, you might not have the resources of a *Fortune* 500 company, and as an employee, you might not have complete autonomy, but each of us gets to decide what we have to say and how we're going to go about it. The ingenuity and ideas, sweat and skills of individuals are the engines of our corporations and communities. Our collective prosperity depends on each of us taking that first small step toward owning our story and the unique contribution we can make.

Australian airline Qantas employs 30,000 people, and every one of those people is a representative of the company's story. The woman clearing tables in the Qantas airport lounge is almost invisible to the preoccupied travellers that she cleans up after. People are anxious to charge their devices, grab a bite to eat and catch their flights. The lounge attendant scrapes plates of half-eaten food and piles them on a trolley to take back to the kitchen. Sometimes people stop to ask her where they can get a drink or an extra spoon, but they don't really see her because she's on the periphery. As far from the centre as it's possible to be.

She spots a man waiting for his flight, his feet awkwardly resting on a table, balancing a MacBook on his knee. It's a bad angle to work at, but at least he's got a power outlet and WiFi. The attendant stops what she's doing to bring a low stool for the man to rest his feet on. She helps to turn his chair so he won't strain his back while he works. Then she silently returns to wiping tables and clearing plates as the travellers busy themselves all around her. She may not always get to choose the work, but how she does it is a choice. Her decisions and actions reflect the truth about the company story.

Ten years ago I lived at the edge of the world—as far away from another city as it's possible to be—in beautiful Perth, Western Australia. It was there that I started my writing career. I was frustrated when one friend after another who wanted business advice failed to take the next step. They loved talking about their ideas for changing the world, but they stalled at the place where they had to decide to grasp the opportunity that was theirs for the taking. So, I decided to stop telling and start showing. I began blogging about those ideas and putting them out into the world for free. My intention was to find the people like you who were ready to run with them.

When I began writing, I had no idea if anyone would want to read what I wrote or how much it was possible to contribute from a distance, but I decided to try. Several books and a community of loyal readers and doers later, I'm glad I did. I hope that by the end of this book, you will be ready to go from understanding your value to deciding to tell and live your story, so that you can look back in two years' or ten years' time and be glad you did.

INTRODUCTION

*'[S]uccess is like a mountain that keeps
growing ahead of you as you hike it... and
there's the very real danger that "succeeding"
will take up your whole life, while the big
questions go untended.'*
*—George Saunders, convocation speech for the
Syracuse University class of 2013*

The story broke on 15th September 2015. It was less of a story and more of a scandal—the biggest deception ever discovered in auto-making history. The United States Environmental Protection Agency had evidence that the world's largest car manufacturer had been deliberately cheating on emissions tests for at least six years. Eleven million diesel cars that had been marketed as 'clean' in order to boost sales and profits had been fitted with 'defeat devices'—software that would give compliant emissions readings under test conditions, but actually allow the cars to emit forty times the allowed amount of nitrogen oxides under normal driving conditions. Not only did these vehicles fail to meet regulatory requirements, but they also were emitting pollutants at levels considered to be harmful to public health.

As news stories spread, speculation escalated and stock prices tumbled; 40 percent ($30 billion) was wiped from Volkswagen's value in a matter of days. VW's CEO, Martin Winterkorn, resigned, saying that he wasn't aware he'd done anything wrong, but he recognised that 'millions of people across the world trust our brands, our cars and our technologies', and he was 'deeply sorry we have broken this trust'.

Volkswagen's new CEO, Matthias Mueller, later explained that the emission compliance issue was a technical problem that arose because the company 'had some targets for [their] technical engineers, and they solved this problem and reached targets with some software solutions which [weren't] compatible [with] the American law'. This seeming lack of insight and reluctance to shoulder blame did not go down well with customers or the media, and the statement was later clarified.

The cost to VW in fines and compensation alone is estimated to be in excess of $20 billion. The reality is that the scandal cost them much more in lost reputation. The emissions fraud wasn't the work of one person—a lapse in judgement of a lone wolf trying to meet a target. It was a systemic failure in the company, akin to a mutation in human DNA that allows a cancer to run rampant through a body. The company once known as the maker of 'the people's car' had lost touch with its identity and failed its people. They had forgotten who they were.

Two weeks to the day from the breaking of the emissions scandal, the world's first all-electric SUV, the Model X, was unveiled in California by Elon Musk, the CEO of Tesla Motors. The fledgling automaker had not yet sold 100,000 cars in its lifetime. Less than two years after the first Model X cars took to the road, *Consumer Reports* ranked Tesla as the top American car brand and eighth in the world. To put that achievement and Volkswagen's material advantage into perspective, Volkswagen Group, founded in 1937, was seventh on the *Fortune* Global 500 list. The company produces more vehicles in two days than Tesla did in all of 2016.

Why would people at a company like Volkswagen, with virtually unlimited resources—assets of €381.9 billion, plus talent, expertise and brand equity—risk everything by taking an illegal shortcut? What enabled the smaller, less-well-resourced team at Tesla Motors to be so innovative? Apart from the obvious differences in resources and longevity, what distinguishes each of these brands from the other is the business philosophies upon which they are built.

In its 2011 annual report to shareholders, Volkswagen declared, 'The main goal of the group's strategy is for Volkswagen to become the economic and ecological leader of the global automotive industry.' The company's goal was to beat the competition and be number one. It's clear from the report that the single bottom line was the leadership's key driver. Volkswagen defined four objectives that would enable them to become 'the most successful and fascinating enterprise of the global automotive industry by 2018'. Innovation, increased sales, increased pre-tax return on sales, and being a 'top employer' were listed as the means by which they would achieve this goal. It seems now that the desire to be innovative was only a means to an end, rather than a reason to strive for excellence. We're left wondering where, or if, happy customers fit into their plans.

As the dust was settling on the emissions scandal, Herbert Diess, CEO of the Volkswagen brand, reiterated Volkswagen's competitive worldview in an interview: 'We see Volkswagen as the company that can stop Tesla, because we have abilities Tesla doesn't have today.' In 2017, Patrick McGee reported in *The Financial Times* that Diess confirmed the company's intention to go after a big slice of the electric car market. 'Anything Tesla can do, we can surpass', he said. He also confirmed that Volkswagen aimed to stop Tesla from getting a foothold in the market for more-affordable electric cars: 'It's our ambition, with our new architecture, to stop them there, to rein them in. We are confident that in this new world we will become a market leader.'

It seems that Volkswagen's narrative and identity still centre around its targets and capabilities, the ability to dominate and the goal of being number one.

In stark contrast, the Tesla team is working towards its vision for the future. Since the brand's inception, the company has been committed to making a contribution to the wider world. Tesla's people have always been united around a single mission: 'to accelerate the world's transition to sustainable transport'. This mission was updated in 2016, changing 'transport' to 'energy'. Elon Musk published his 'secret Tesla Motors master plan' online in 2006 for the world to see. The company's contribution, aspirations and values inform the strategy he laid out at that time. Here's an excerpt:

*As you know, the initial product of Tesla Motors is a
high performance electric sports car called the Tesla
Roadster. However, some readers may not be aware
of the fact that our long term plan is to build a wide
range of models, including affordably priced family
cars. This is because the overarching purpose of Tesla
Motors (and the reason I am funding the company)
is to help expedite the move from a mine-and-burn
hydrocarbon economy towards a solar electric economy,
which I believe to be the primary, but not exclusive,
sustainable solution. ...*

So, in short, the master plan is:

*Build sports car
Use that money to build an affordable [electric] car
Use that money to build an even more affordable
[electric] car
While doing above, also provide zero emission electric
power generation options.*

Prior to the emissions scandal, the engineering team
at Volkswagen lived in fear of being unable to meet tough
innovation deadlines, while the people at Tesla were aspiring
to become the company that would change the world.
Ironically, in its attempt to catch up to Tesla, Volkswagen is
undoubtedly helping them to realise their vision to accelerate
the transition to sustainable energy.

What went wrong at Volkswagen? Why did a team of
presumably smart, dedicated people, with a legacy to uphold
and access to unlimited resources, lose their way? Those of us

on the outside looking in will never know the exact details about the errors in human judgement that caused the crisis. But we can take a step back and see how the company's philosophy and internal narrative shaped its identity, culture and strategy. We can learn from the mistakes of the past.

TWO KINDS OF COMPANIES

Whether it's articulated or not, every business is driven by one of two philosophies. A company is either competition-driven or story-driven.

The competition-driven company is reactive to the marketplace and prioritises beating its competitors and racking up profits. It identifies with the capitalist ideal and is intent on keeping score. The people who lead competition-driven organisations seek to dominate the market and maximise shareholder value. They care about increasing market share, boosting the single bottom line and raising their status as 'the leader' in their category. Their goal is to win.

COMPETITION-DRIVEN COMPANY
Reactive
Competitors + Winning

In contrast, the story-driven company is responsive to customers and prioritises having a clear sense of purpose and identity. It makes little reference to the competition and is intent on creating an impact. The people who work there derive a deep sense of meaning from their work because they know their company exists to do more than simply make a profit. The leaders of story-driven companies (big and small) have clear visions for the future they want to see, and they inspire their teams to join them on the journey to creating that future. They often succeed by doing things that can't be measured or are not immediately scalable. Story-driven companies have a positive impact on their customers and society. They thrive by making the connection between their purpose and prosperity. Their goal is to make a difference.

STORY-DRIVEN COMPANY
Responsive
Customers + Mattering

The positive and negative things that happen in and around a company are almost always a direct result of its philosophy. A company's philosophy shapes its identity and its internal and external narratives. Conversely, just as our personal narratives can influence who we become and how our lives evolve, a company's narrative also influences its identity and has a direct impact on what its leaders and employees think, believe, say and do. This identity inevitably shapes the culture. That's why leaders have to take responsibility when things go wrong, even if they were not directly involved in the wrongdoing: they helped to create a culture where people believed that the wrong thing was the right thing to do.

What's the secret to building a great company?

Great companies have something in common: they don't try to matter by winning. They win by mattering. The people who build them know what they stand for and act on those beliefs. What they think, say and do are always in alignment. Their story is consistent. Great companies rise to our expectations by being who they said they would be.

In a commercial world, we are conditioned to compete for tangible near-term gains in the name of success. But whether as an individual or as a brand, you can't thrive if you spend the majority of your time competing with and comparing yourself to others. Differentiation happens when you authentically amplify the best of you—discovering how to be more of who you are, rather than finding ways to be a version of the competition.

It's hard to do work you're proud of if you're focused on crushing the competition or making the next million. There is an alternative, though: you can harness the power of your unique identity to build a brand that matters.

The story you live and the identity you inhabit are always a choice. You don't have to operate with the default setting that always, and without question, greedily pays homage to the metric of 'more'. You can choose to create a career or a company that enables you to do work you're proud of—and that prospers in the service of others.

THE DOWNSIDE OF PLAYING TO WIN

When it comes to business strategy, competition-driven companies behave like players in a soccer match. They play to win—acting as if there are only ninety minutes to affect the result. They engage in what philosopher James Carse calls a 'finite game'. As Carse explains, 'Since finite games are played to be won, players make every move in a game in order to win. Whatever is not done in the interest of winning is not part of the game.'

In the lead-up to the emissions scandal, when the leaders at Volkswagen prioritised beating the competition and becoming number one in their industry, they were playing a finite game. Their tactics demonstrated the commitment to a competition-driven philosophy. The impatience to hit near-term targets in order to deliver value for shareholders meant that shortcuts were taken.

It's inevitable that when a company identifies itself as being at war with the competition, it creates a 'play to win' culture, where the emphasis is largely on making the numbers go up. The entire focus shifts towards being the team that gets the most balls in the back of the net by whatever means necessary. This approach leaves little room for answering the hard questions about the company's contribution and impact over time. In Volkswagen's case, even when sales rebound, the fallout from 'playing to win' will likely tarnish its reputation, affecting customers' perception of the brand and employee morale for years to come. It's not *that* you win but *how* you win that matters. What you sacrifice on the way can mean that ultimately you lose.

Contrast Volkswagen's philosophy with Tesla's. By building a story-driven company, Musk is playing what Carse describes as 'an infinite game'. *An infinite game is played 'for the purpose of continuing the play'.* Musk's intention is to stay in the game. His strategy is to build companies that can create a bigger impact tomorrow and thus become more relevant in the future, rather than to only fixate on today's metrics of success.

In a capitalist culture, it can be hard to identify yourself as an infinite-game player when the majority of businesses have their eyes on a different prize. But the companies we believe in and support with our attention, money and loyalty have proven that it's possible to thrive by adopting this more visionary business philosophy. Your company's identity and internal narrative aren't just a set of guiding principles to believe in; as you'll see later in the book, they can also be part of a long-term strategy that powers your ongoing success.

REDEFINING GREATNESS

By most conventional measures of success, Uber is a great company. Going from a standing start in 2009 to a valuation of $70 billion early in 2017, the maker of the ride-hailing app became the most valuable private technology company in the world. Uber achieved the kind of growth many companies dream of, and yet the string of scandals related to discrimination against and harassment of female employees in 2017 tell the story of a company culture that's broken. These events eventually led to the resignation of Uber's co-founder and CEO, Travis Kalanick.

According to Uber's new CEO, Dara Khosrowshahi, 'winning gave some excuses for bad behavior.' He acknowledges that while Uber was scaling as a business, 'it wasn't necessarily scaling in terms of culture.'

We frequently witness similar missteps in seemingly successful competition-driven companies that are striving for and attaining our culture's current narrow definition of greatness.

In our Western world of abundance and privilege, greatness is a game of comparison that drives us to achieve more. Bigger wins, more sales, hockey-stick growth charts, increased market share, scale, power and influence. Permanently higher highs that inevitably end in compromise.

We have created a culture where we're not winning unless someone else is less-than or losing.

We're constantly trying to get our arms around what it means to be successful. Success is always something we're aiming to achieve at some point in the future, not something we feel we can experience in the moment. Success is never now. And we often aspire to attaining it without understanding what it means for us personally. Is it a dollar figure? Status? Awards? Accomplishments? Accolades? Something else? The traditional trappings of success (interesting that they're called trappings) are easy to point to—stellar career, big house, nice car, exotic holidays and maybe even five minutes of fame. But if I asked you right now how you will know when you've achieved it, you'd probably struggle to give an immediate answer. Even when we think we know what we're working towards, our actions from day to day don't always support our answers.

The pursuit of 'more' often leads us down blind alleys towards the dead ends we're trying to avoid. The startup forsakes revenue or foregoes a sustainable business model so it can scale rapidly. Corporations prioritise shareholder value over customer satisfaction. The CEO compromises his values and does whatever it takes to reach an arbitrary target that's been set for the quarter. We strive, achieve, reset, rinse and repeat, never quite getting to wherever 'there' is.

The irony, of course, is that the people and success stories we're drawn to and try to emulate are aspirational precisely because they stand for something and don't necessarily take the fast or easy route to 'more'. From Amazon to Apple, Branson to Blakely, those who are pioneers in their fields consciously take a path they believe is worth walking. For them, success is now—the alignment of thoughts, beliefs, intentions and actions. The journey is part of their success.

While it seems like a daunting task, it's possible for us as individuals to redefine greatness by changing how we measure success—by replacing our winner-takes-more worldview with one that requires us to ask if we're doing work we're proud of. We each get to decide what it means to be great. Moment to moment and day by day, we can deliberately choose to do only the things we'll be proud to have done and to create the future we want to see. We start by deciding who we are—what philosophy and values will guide us and our companies—and by investing the time to reflect on the unique contribution we can make. If we want to prioritise people over profits and impact over dividends, we need to choose carefully what we will measure each day.

MOVE INTENTIONALLY AND BUILD THINGS

Who could or would argue against doing work you're proud of or creating the future you want to see? What we can debate, though, is the best way to go about building a successful business and thriving culture. Nobody sets out to create a product or company that's mediocre or, worse still, one that causes harm. We all want to do work that matters. We start every day with that intention. And yet, despite our best efforts, we falter. We sometimes take shortcuts. Say things we don't mean. Make promises we're unlikely to keep. Take on projects that don't resonate with our values, and do things we wouldn't want to put our names to. Even if we do manage to do work we're proud of, it is often hard to scale with integrity.

Why do we act in ways that are incongruent with doing our best work? Why is it so hard to prioritise opportunities and create the right culture? Are we afraid of missing the boat? Have we grown too fast? Underestimated the challenges? Hired the wrong people? Are we worried that admitting mistakes will cost us our jobs? Has our self-worth become wrapped up in getting a promotion or making the next million? Perhaps we've spread ourselves too thin, by trying to do too much, too fast, with too little. Or maybe we are just limited by a conventional view of success.

When we constantly pursue and prioritise 'more' above 'meaning', we take wrong turns, box ourselves in, self-sabotage or make unhelpful plans. We become less sure about the best way to achieve our goals, and we make the wrong decisions on the fly. These mistakes happen when we haven't done the groundwork of understanding our narrative—getting clear about why our business exists and what difference we're here to create, for whom. We need a clear purpose and vision that help us to make stepwise progress to a thoughtfully chosen goal—one that isn't simply represented by a dollar figure.

Visionary entrepreneurs and successful companies consistently act in alignment with their values because they know who they are and who they want to become. They are guided by an internal narrative that reminds them why they do what they do and where it's important to head next. This enables them to zoom out and take a 360-degree view before deciding which path to take next. That opportunity is open to every one of us.

Your story has the potential to be more than superficial marketing veneer applied in order to sell average products or to manipulate people into making decisions they later regret—both of which marketing often, sadly, consigns 'story' to. Your story can be a reminder to ask the big questions that will guide you, and make the small choices that sustain you. Your identity can ground you—serving as a reminder to be intentional about the work you do and deliberate about creating the future you want to see.

PART ONE
The Reason

'The critical question is not "How can I achieve?" but "What can I contribute?"'
—Jim Collins, reflecting on what he learned from Peter Drucker, in the foreword to *The Daily Drucker: 366 Days of Insight and Motivation for Getting the Right Things Done*

What's the first thing we do when we decide to start a business or embark on a new project? We might register a domain name, get a logo designed, build a website, canvas our friends for their opinions, have a strategy meeting with colleagues, conduct a focus group, build a minimum viable product, pitch investors, create a marketing campaign, launch, pivot, scale. While we're busy with the tactical stuff, we often skip the important first step—of reflecting deeply about the reason our idea or project needs to exist and the change we're trying to create. This first step is harder than it seems, because asking these deeper questions makes us feel vulnerable to failure. We'd rather press on unenlightened, doing fun, practical and easy things that help us to feel like we're making progress. We prefer to fix mistakes as we go rather than to sit with the uncomfortable unknowns about our ambitions. Having ideas is fun. Understanding what makes them relevant today or significant tomorrow, and why you're the person to move them forward, is work.

At the heart of every good idea or great business is a clear sense of purpose and a vision for the future its creator wants to see. Research into neuroplasticity and how the mind changes the brain has proven what celebrated thinkers like Victor Frankl, author of *Man's Search for Meaning*, have intuitively known: we are more likely to make progress when we believe in the significance of what we're doing. In one study carried out by researchers at Stanford University, students who were encouraged to view tedious academic tasks as stepping stones to college, rather than as means to an end, found learning more meaningful.

If having a sense of purpose can improve your chances of success, it's vital to imagine how what you're working on creates change and to articulate your reasons for wanting to do it. Why you? Why this? Why now? Why for them? Why there? Why that way and not this? What's your story and how will you stay true to it?

After many years of practicing medicine, my husband, Moyez, decided to experiment with the layout of the consultation room. He wanted to see if small changes, that could be easily implemented by anyone, would benefit the patient. He limited himself to changing just one thing at a time. Moyez moved the big, comfy chair—the one that's usually reserved for the doctor—out from behind the desk and, after greeting the patient, invited him or her to take a seat in it. Moyez then sat in the standard-issue patient seating, alongside the patient. In our culture, the big chair is a symbol of power. From the aircraft to the corner office, the big chair is reserved for the person 'in charge' and thus in control. The invitation to sit in that chair gave patients the sense that they could influence their health outcomes. It was also an outward sign of Moyez's capacity for empathy. This tiny tweak changed the whole dynamic of the consultation, helping patients to feel more empowered and less anxious. They became more open and felt that they were heard and understood.

When Moyez told an older, non-medical colleague about his 'big chair' experiment, the colleague stopped him short. 'What's your story?' he said. 'You didn't learn how to do that at medical school.' Moyez told him the story of landing in Birmingham at the age of ten, as an economic migrant from East Africa en route to Ireland with his mother and younger brother, to meet his father who had a job there. He remembers being taken into a side room and being made to strip naked by immigration officers to have a health check before being allowed to continue on to his destination. Forty years later, he still recalls how vulnerable he felt. That experience is part of the reason he is a better doctor and a better mentor to medical students today. Our formative experiences—the stories that were the making of us—can influence us (and how we choose to go about our lives and work) long afterward.

Without a narrative compass, our creative endeavours, companies and cultures break down, and we become faint carbon copies of something that's gone before. Our story illuminates the dark corners where only we can go. It's our story that guides us.

MEANING IS A COMPETITIVE ADVANTAGE

In the 1950s and '60s, when my parents were entering the workforce, they created value by working with their hands in an Industrial Economy. Workers manufactured and moved things that would be consumed. In the era of the Information Economy, we began using our heads to produce value. We learned to use computers to design, code and connect. Today we're seeing a powerful shift towards the building of the Meaning Economy, where the brands and businesses that thrive are the ones that enable us to work with our hearts as well as our heads and hands.

Unlike my parents, who worked for a brown envelope containing the money that would put food on the table each week, many of us are not simply working to survive. Our work is also how we get a sense of fulfilment. We want to feel proud of the work we do and the companies where we do it. We want it to count for something—to be meaningful. As Professor Dan Ariely reminds us in his book *Payoff*, meaning's 'essential quality has to do with having a sense of purpose, value, and impact—of being involved in something bigger than the self'.

The Meaning Economy has also created a new kind of customer who is drawn to brands that share and enable them to express their values. We know that how we spend our money and which causes we champion are votes for the future we want to see. We support businesses that are generous and mindful of the impact they make. We're moving towards the formulation of a new value equation—one that rewards work that is carried out with heart and rewards businesses that are driven by purpose before profits. A company's purpose is sometimes unarticulated or buried deep in the company's DNA, but it's still possible to sense and experience it.

In our quest for success, we spend the majority of our time chasing the kind of growth we believe quickly bolsters some tangible metric. We aim to expand our reach, convert more customers and overtake our competitors—sometimes at the expense of doing what's right or what lights us up. We often ignore the things that motivate us to do the great work, things that will, ironically, enable us to expand our reach, attract more customers, be competitive and feel fulfilled. When we prioritise meaning in our companies and communities, it becomes easier to have authentic conversations with our stakeholders and to be honest with our customers.

Putting contribution before profits is still an underrated business strategy. Look around you at the companies you admire, the brands you are loyal to and the businesses you support. They likely have one thing in common. These businesses don't simply exist to turn a profit—they are contributing to your community, the wellbeing of their teams and the betterment of the world, sometimes indirectly. In cities and towns, cafés have become inviting workspaces, and twenty-four-hour convenience stores have become places where the homeless can warm up on bitter winter nights. Vinyl record and book stores can be cultural hubs. And conscious-clothing retailers lead cultural shifts.

According to Robert Safian, editor of *Fast Company*, 'an experiment is under way in parts of corporate America to redefine the role of business in society.' We are beginning to question more deeply the role that business plays in adding value to our lives, communities and cultures. We're seeing a move towards business leaders questioning their responsibility to the world and being more explicit about the reasons their companies should exist and the future they are intent on creating.

Increasing awareness has long been the goal of every business, but today our thinking and priorities are shifting. In a world where it's easy to be cheaper and faster than the competition, we now recognise the limitations of attention and the power of affinity. Humans are wired to do what feels good, and what feels good to customers right now is to use their choices and purchasing power to support the building of a better tomorrow. That means buying from businesses that are motivated by generosity and contribution, and that have an inclusive view of the economy rather than a selfish one.

NARRATIVE AND IDENTITY

'Story' is defined as 'a narrative, either true or fictitious, in prose or verse, designed to interest, amuse, or instruct the hearer or reader'. This limiting definition sells 'story' short. Traditionally, in business and career development, we've primarily used our stories as communication tactics—ways to get people to see us—while overlooking the opportunity to leverage them to help us see ourselves more clearly. Far from just being a way to differentiate us, our stories can help us to decide, plan, lead, sell, inspire, influence, persuade, rally, create value, build trust, foster connection and succeed by building better, more purposeful organisations and lives. Our stories can shape who we are.

Psychology Professor Dan McAdams provides us with a simple model for understanding how as humans, our personality develops over time, in three layers. The foundation is who we are at birth and how we develop in early life—our traits. The second layer is our goals and values—what we believe and strive for as we get older. The final layer is our stories—what we choose to remember about our past and how we make it meaningful now and in the future. These layers of our personality come into play at different times in our lives and are linked to McAdams's theory of narrative identity. He says that we are born actors, begin to develop agency around the age of eight and become authors of our stories in our late teens onwards. McAdams proposes that a person's identity is formed by integrating life experiences into an internalised, evolving story that provides him or her with a sense of purpose. We make sense of who we are by piecing together stories from our reconstructed past, perceived present and imagined future. As Professor McAdams explains, 'In personality psychology, what mainly counts when it comes to the idea of a life story is the narrator's subjective understanding of how he or she came to be the person he or she is becoming— that is, the person's narrative identity.'

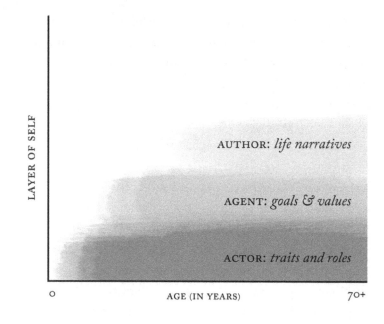

the 3 layers of self, developing over time

credit: *Professor Dan P. McAdams*

Far from simply being a rigid history or timeline of facts, our story about who we once were, are now and could become in the future can evolve over time. Like a master weaver, we subjectively select threads from what we remember of our past and combine them to create a narrative that reflects our present priorities and future goals. We fashion a story we want to live into. In this way, our autobiographical memory guides our behaviour and helps us to solve problems, maintain intimacy and create social bonds. It also allows us to create and preserve our sense of identity and to have insights that can help us grow.

WHO DO YOU THINK YOU ARE?

As business leaders, we've learned how to become better technical storytellers, for the purpose of marketing our products and services, by borrowing from what the best writers know about Joseph Campbell's 'hero's journey'. Our customer is seen as someone who needs a guide on a quest. We (our businesses, products and services) become that guide, helping them reach their goals or fulfil their unmet needs. We are less clear about how to make sense of the connection between our story—our unique identity and the day-to-day decisions about what we stand for—and how our principles will guide us as we plan for the future.

The story-driven company thrives because its people have a collective narrative identity that gives them a sense of purpose and creates a cohesive culture. When you know where you came from and where you're going, decisions become easier. You know which clients are a good fit and which ones are not. You have a way to filter options and make decisions that will get you to where you want to go without compromising on your values.

As Robert Safian, editor of *Fast Company* magazine, points out, 'companies are increasingly seeking to align their commercial activities with larger social and cultural values' because they know it's good for business. It also benefits the prosperity of a company (of any size) when its founders, leaders and employees have a sense that they're contributing to something bigger than themselves. That contribution doesn't have to be centred around building a social enterprise or donating part of the profits to good causes, as brands like Warby Parker and TOMS Shoes do. Your company can create ripples in your local community and beyond.

I've worked with hundreds of entrepreneurs and business leaders who have built successful story-driven businesses. Some of my clients started out with nothing but an idea for solving an unmet need, and others are helping to accelerate growth in billion-dollar corporations. I've consulted with dentists and jewellery designers, publishers and technology companies, builders and café owners, and I can tell you that every business idea starts from a place of wanting to contribute something. I have yet to meet a single person who has a hand in building a business who doesn't want to make a meaningful impact on more than the bottom line. We humans are wired for connection and contribution. We thrive when we get the opportunity to do both. This is why there is an element of fundamental good in every business backstory. You just have to stop for long enough and retrace your steps to find it. Your company's origins and ethos—your intention and aspiration to create an impact on the world and in the lives of the people your business touches—shape your identity and your strategy. You already have a story; it's how you choose to interpret and use it that's key to your success.

A couple of years ago, I had the privilege of working with the leadership team at ASSA ABLOY Hospitality, when they were rebranding their established Vingcard brand. If you've stayed in a hotel room, you've likely used their products and services. ASSA ABLOY makes the recodeable keycards that unlock millions of hotel room doors around the globe every day. We began the journey not by focussing on where the company was going, but by retracing the steps on its journey to now. What were their roots? Why had the company started? How did their backstory influence the work they did today and how might it affect their aspirations for the future? As we began to dig deeper, some of the people who'd been with the company for years fondly retold the founder's story. A lone Norwegian lock engineer, Tor Sørnes, who was a big fan of the American singer Connie Francis, heard the news that she had been attacked in her hotel bedroom while she was on tour. He was so moved by her story that he felt compelled to create a more secure way of locking hotel rooms so people would feel safe when they travelled. It was from these humble beginnings, with one man's drive to contribute, that a successful global business was launched.

The most committed entrepreneurs and successful organisations know how important and powerful understanding their narratives can be. What drives Elon Musk, for example, is the ability to be useful, to secure a good future for the human race and to create things that make a difference to a large number of people. Musk is clear about what he and his team aspire to do over the next ten years. His aspiration to move to a sustainable energy economy, one that helps to avert the collapse of civilisation, is the reason they are executing on a story-driven strategy to:

Create stunning solar roofs with integrated battery storage, expand the electric vehicle product line to address all major segments, develop a self-driving capability that is 10X safer than manual and enable your car to make money for you when you aren't using it.

If someone were to ask you about your work or your business, you'd probably tell them your job title and give them a rundown of what you make, whom you serve, and where and how long you've been doing it. It's unlikely that you'd begin by telling them about your purpose and vision and why these are important in the grand scheme of things. What's at the heart of your story? What's the reason you got out of bed this morning? It isn't just to make more money for your boss or the need to sell some average product you made. It's the deep, often unspoken, desire to change something you care about changing and the belief that it's possible. Sometimes we forget why we started, and in doing so we miss the opportunity to harness the power of our unique identity and our story.

THE NARRATIVE EFFECT

We are faced with hundreds of choices every day—decisions sometimes so small we hardly recognise them as conscious choices at all. Will we hit the gym or the snooze button, check Facebook or meditate, eat porridge or an Egg McMuffin? And that's just before breakfast. The decisions we make are subconsciously primed by our biases—our inclinations and opinions, worldviews and prejudices. These biases form the basis of the stories we believe about ourselves, the world and our place in it. For example, researchers have shown that our innate desire to reciprocate makes us more likely to buy cheese at the deli after we've been offered a sample. It's also been proven that our tendency to conform can make us change the correct answer to a test question to the incorrect one if we know that the majority of people taking the test also chose the wrong answer. Studies into neuroplasticity—how the brain can reorganise itself and form new connections— have demonstrated that changes in the brain don't occur only in response to disease or injury. The brain can also adapt to our thoughts and feelings, as psychologist Carol Dweck found; our underlying beliefs about intelligence, learning and failure can affect our choices, behaviour and performance.

How can we make more conscious decisions? How does our internal narrative change our behaviour? And how does this decision-making process play out in organisations?

Our personal values act as a compass, helping us to behave in ways that are congruent with who we believe we are and who we aspire to be. Furthermore, it's almost impossible to make decisions that don't reinforce the story about who you believe yourself to be. If you're the kind of person who believes reducing waste can help mitigate the effects of global warming, then you won't buy single-use plastic water bottles, and if you're a vegetarian, there's no way you'd order rump steak at a restaurant. Our choices, as they accumulate over time, strengthen our personal narrative.

Similarly, a company culture—the values system agreed upon by the group—drives the organisation's decisions and behaviours. We see examples of culture informing business strategy all the time. Steve Jobs delayed the release of the Macintosh because the chips in the circuit board didn't line up neatly. This was something the user would never see, but as Jobs told his team, 'You will know.' Jobs knew that his engineers were driven by a sense of pride in their work. He believed they should and would do whatever it took to turn out their best once he reflected their values-based standards back to them. In contrast, the engineers at Volkswagen were so driven by a culture of fear that they chose to cheat rather than admit failure.

The fashion brand Everlane's culture centres around radical transparency. That translates into a particular narrative and worldview that lead to unusual strategic decisions. Everlane's website clearly displays a breakdown of prices for every item they sell, so customers can see the cost of materials, labour, and transport and see the company's profit on the cashmere sweater they are about to buy. Everlane also publishes stories about the factories they use, including details about where they're located, how the company found them, who runs them and what materials they use. These stories are accompanied by rich imagery and sometimes videos of the craftspeople who work there.

Whatever our goals are, we must have a plan and a process for achieving them. Good decisions are a critical part of any strategy. What classifies a decision as the right one depends on the outcomes we optimise our organisations to create. Those outcomes are as individual as the people who want to achieve them. If we are aiming to be this and not that, then we need to make choices that are consistent with this and not with that. We must act in accordance with who we say we are and use our narrative to guide us to become the people who build the kind of organisations we want to exist.

THE BUSINESS OF STORY

Worldwide ad spending for 2017 is expected to reach almost $584 billion. That's an increase of 7.3 percent from the previous year. We invest extraordinary sums of money and disproportionate amounts of time in trying to get people to notice us. We're used to leveraging the power of storytelling commercially to attract attention or gain an advantage over our competitors. We devote tremendous resources to what has been called 'the war on attention' in the hope that more people will remember our brand, ignore the competition and choose to do business with us instead. This attention-getting strategy not only sells storytelling and our companies short; it also means that we continually have to reinvent ourselves, with bigger and better stories, to stay in the more-eyeballs game. The irony is, no business ever died from a shortage of attention. Companies and ideas fail because of a lack of resonance with the people they seek to serve.

So why are we still hoping to conjure brand equity in an instant out of thin air? We know people will pay more for a running shoe with a tick on the side than one without, because of the expectation and meaning associated with the Nike brand. And who doesn't want their company to be more meaningful and valuable? This desire to create and communicate value, in an attempt to compete for customer mindshare, is often the initial driver to get better at brand storytelling. And it's also the reason we're under-utilising one of our most precious resources—the power of our identity.

There's an elephant in the marketing room and I'd like us to call it out. Here goes: by setting out to find and tell the *right* story, we lose sight of the *real* story—the truth about who we are. We mistakenly assume that marketing is about adapting our story according to what most people want to hear. We go off in search of an angle that will attract the most attention today. As a result, we don't devote enough time and resources to reflecting on how we can resonate with the right people—just as we are. We fail to harness the true potential of our narrative.

Pretending is exhausting. When we pretend, we not only miss the opportunity to deeply connect with the right audience in a way that gives us a sustainable advantage; more important, we're left feeling as unfulfilled as they are disappointed.

When our ancestors first crossed the desert with salt and gold to barter with strangers who couldn't speak their language, they practiced 'silent trade'. Value was communicated and understood without either buyer or seller having to utter a word. Trust was implicit in every transaction. Communities grew and societies blossomed on the back of both connection and commerce, in a world built on promises.

Today we spend a lot of our time *telling* people why they should trust us. Marketing tactics change weekly. More disruptors enter the marketplace daily. Your colleagues' and competitors' 'wins' are posted hourly on TechCrunch, LinkedIn and VentureBeat. Your company metrics are made public and shareholder value dissected. Your competitors gain ground, hacking their way to growth while you're still getting to grips with your strategy. It's not hard to get thrown off course or sense that you're being left behind. What should you devote your energy and resources to next? Which new social media platform is worth investigating and why? Should you attend networking events or adopt a new growth strategy? What will your return on investment be? And what's the point anyhow? The new tools and tactics are easy to learn and automate; what's harder, scarcer and more useful is setting the intention that guides the work you do, the service you deliver, the attitude you adopt and the meaning you hope to create.

The first step to resonating with customers is to stop pretending and have a clear sense of our own identity. Instead of just using storytelling as a marketing tactic, we need to do what our ancestors did for millennia—allow our stories to guide our actions, deepen our understanding and create meaning and belonging. In a world of abundance, value is increasingly created by experiences and interactions that are not easily replicated. The old tactics of convincing our way to the sale with billboards and banner ads are not working so well anymore. *Today we differentiate by doing.* The more deliberate we can be about acting in alignment with our intentions, the more we stand out.

The growing number of B Corps and the sentiment among CEOs that it's becoming 'more important to have a strong corporate purpose that's reflected in [a company's] values, culture and behaviours' are evidence that some quarters of the business community are shifting towards understanding how to run profitable companies while also doing the right thing. We still have work to do until the overwhelming majority of businesses think and act this way. B Corps are 'for-profit companies certified by the non-profit B Lab to meet rigorous standards of social and environmental performance, accountability, and transparency'. As of this writing, there are 2,100 Certified B Corps from fifty countries in over 130 industries 'working together toward one unifying goal: to redefine success in business', thus making business a force for good. These businesses are 'measuring what matters', tracking their positive contributions with like-minded peers. We're going back to our roots and understanding anew how potent our promises can be.

Before you write a line of code or a word of copy, before you apply for that promotion or plan your growth strategy, and before you create your next marketing campaign or send that sales email, you need to understand what's driving your story. Where are the roots that will enable you to grow healthy branches that bear fruit? How will you show, not just tell? What promises are you intending to keep?

STORY AS STRATEGY

At its simplest, a strategy is a plan for achieving a goal—a bird's-eye view of the path that will take us from where we are now to where we want to go.

It's important to understand the distinction between strategy and tactics if we're to elevate 'story' in our organisations and use it as more than just a communications tool. If a strategy is the path to your goal, tactics are the specific steps you take as you navigate that path. Imagine your business purpose and vision as a mountain peak. Your strategy is the route map—the path you choose that's going to get you up that mountain. Tactics are the steps you take on the journey to advance your way along that chosen path towards the summit, thus realising your vision.

PURPOSE AND VISION—Where you're going and why.

STRATEGY—How you're going to get there.

TACTICS—What you do along the way.

'Story' is frequently used as a tactic to attract the attention of customers. We agonise for weeks over perfect taglines, choosing logo designs and articulating features and benefits, often without fully understanding how or even if those tactics (the things we spend most of our time doing) are helping us to get where we want to go. By failing to *also* see our narrative as part of our strategy, we're missing the opportunity to get clear on our purpose, differentiate ourselves from the competition and create affinity with the right customers. Differentiation begins by showing, not just telling, and every action should serve the purpose of advancing us towards our goal. We make better decisions when we understand why we're making them.

When Chinese entrepreneur Jack Ma founded the e-commerce, retail and technology conglomerate Alibaba Group in 1999, his company's purpose was to 'make it easy to do business anywhere'. His vision: to 'build the future infrastructure of commerce'. Ma envisioned being a 'company that lasts at least 102 years'. He believed that Alibaba would succeed by creating the infrastructure that could serve 2 billion consumers, empower 10 million profitable businesses and create 100 million jobs. By 2012, the company's platforms were handling $170 billion in sales. Many Chinese companies competed on price, but Alibaba chose instead to differentiate by offering responsive service.

Ma lowered the barriers to entry for Chinese entrepreneurs by serving individuals and small-business owners. Alibaba made setting up an online store easy and free; associated costs for marketing and technical support were transparent. This strategy enabled the company to create and scale a trusted, secure ecosystem. Alibaba wants to continue investing to strengthen its online payments tool and is making strategic acquisitions with an eye towards global expansion. In the future, the company plans to increasingly leverage cloud computing and big data to further drive customer success. Here is a company that has had a clear understanding of its reason for being and its narrative from day one:

> *Our founders started our company to champion small businesses, in the belief that the Internet would level the playing field by enabling small enterprises to leverage innovation and technology to grow and compete more effectively in the domestic and global economies.*

After the company filed for its IPO in 2014, Ma wrote a letter to employees. Here's part of what he shared with them:

> *We know well we haven't survived because our strategies are farsighted and brilliant, or because our execution is perfect, but because for 15 years we have persevered in our mission of 'making it easier to do business across the world,' because we have insisted on a 'customer first' value system, because we have persisted in believing in the future, and because we have insisted that normal people can do extraordinary things.*

That coherence of values and intention, strategy and operations, has been a key driver of the company's success to this day. In his 2017 letter to shareholders, Ma (now Alibaba Group's executive chairman) said, 'while public shareholders expect us to be profitable, our raison d'être cannot be merely to make money.' He explained how Alibaba could play a bigger role in the development of a thriving Chinese economy:

> *I believe there is a massive opportunity to help alleviate poverty and catalyze economic development in China's rural countryside through technology and innovation. This is our opportunity to showcase what we are really capable of.*

If you want to empower the people who are helping you to build your company, you must have as much clarity as Jack Ma did from the outset about where you're going and why, in order to get there.

THE STORY-DRIVEN FRAMEWORK

The easiest part of telling your story is implementing the tactics—things like articulating your product's features and benefits on a sales page or deciding what colour the logo should be. The hardest part is not only working out the mission, vision and values that are the foundation of your business, but also intentionally living them so you can achieve your goals. You have to begin by getting clear about why your business exists. The very act of questioning your purpose forces you to dig deeper. It invites you to clarify why you wanted to make that particular promise to those particular people in the first place and to create an action plan to deliver on it.

As marketers, we believe that it's our products and words that create value. But it's the intention that informs the development of those products and the crafting of those words that delights people and thus differentiates us. Clarity of intention is where your story starts. Whether it's obvious to us or not, the businesses we are loyal to understand what they're here to do. Examples like Starbucks' aspiration to become 'the third place' and Patagonia's goal of using business to inspire and implement solutions to the environmental crisis demonstrate that customers support businesses who show what they're made of as well as selling what they make.

When your business or organisation is story driven, its aspirations and strategy are underpinned by a clear philosophy that deepens employee engagement and commitment, creates momentum and drives innovation and customer loyalty, thus leading to a solid plan for achieving success. Having a story-driven strategy enables you to adapt in times of change because you understand that your story is bigger than the scene that's playing out in the moment. We get the sense that if climate change were suddenly reversed, Elon Musk would find something else useful to work on for the benefit of society.

Let me introduce you to the simple framework that walks you through the process of building a story-driven brand. The Story-Driven Framework is designed to help you be less reactive and more visionary, less tactical and more strategic. It's a tool you can use personally to guide your career decisions or within teams to inspire engagement and enable progress.

STRATEGY | *align opportunities, plans & behaviour*

VISION | *aspiration for the future*

PURPOSE | *reason to exist*

VALUES | *guiding beliefs*

BACKSTORY | *journey to now*

the story-driven framework

© 2017 Bernadette Jiwa

1. **BACKSTORY:** Your journey to now.

2. **VALUES:** Your guiding beliefs.

3. **PURPOSE:** Your reason to exist.

4. **VISION:** Your aspiration for the future.

5. **STRATEGY:** The alignment of opportunities, plans and behaviour: how you will deliver on your purpose and work towards your aspiration, while staying true to your values.

Being a story-driven company is about more than simply articulating your purpose. It's about staying true to that purpose as you work to realise your vision. Leaders of story-driven companies consistently prioritise the things that will help them achieve their goals while staying true to their values. Every person on the team clearly understands what they are collectively working towards achieving.

Another benefit to building a story-driven company is the enhancement of the company culture and employee motivation and wellbeing. What's less talked about than our business goals, but is increasingly on the radar of business leaders, is the role that having a sense of purpose plays in employee satisfaction and thus productivity. Research by Professor Dan Ariely and his team at Duke University found that we overestimate how motivated people are by money and underestimate the role of meaning at work. People are more motivated, more engaged, happier and more productive when they feel like their work is meaningful.

Let's walk through the Story-Driven Framework by using Jack Ma's company, Alibaba, as an example.

1. BACKSTORY
Journey to now

Jack Ma was born in the city of Hangzhou, China, in 1964 to poor parents who were performers. Jack was a scrawny child who was teased for his size, but he says he was never afraid of fighting the bigger kids. After President Nixon's visit to China in 1972, tourism began to flourish in Hangzhou. As a teenager, Jack learned English by going to a local hotel to meet tourists and offering them free tours in exchange for English lessons. He was rejected for many jobs, including one at Kentucky Fried Chicken. Ma knew that an education would be the key to success for someone like him who didn't have money or connections. He wanted desperately to go to college but failed the college entrance exams twice. Succeeding the third time, he graduated in 1988 and became a teacher. His love of performance made him a natural teacher.

Ma started a Chinese translation business in the '90s, and it was while he was on a business trip to the U.S. in 1995 that he become fascinated by the Internet. He was surprised when he first did an online search for 'beer' and no Chinese results appeared. That fruitless search sparked the idea to start an Internet company in China. His first two ventures failed, but in April 1999 Ma convinced seventeen friends to invest in Alibaba, an online marketplace that would enable Chinese exporters to sell directly to customers. By October of that same year, Alibaba had raised an additional $25 million in venture capital. In 2005, Yahoo invested $1 billion.

Ma's entrepreneurial superpower is his gift for motivating employees. When his company broke the record for the biggest IPO in history, raising $25 billion in September 2014, Ma said, 'Today what we got is not money. What we got is trust from the people.'

2. VALUES
Guiding beliefs

Customer First: The interests of our community of consumers and merchants must be our first priority.

Teamwork: We believe teamwork enables ordinary people to achieve extraordinary things.

Embrace Change: In this fast-changing world, we must be flexible, innovative and ready to adapt to new business conditions in order to survive.

Integrity: We expect our people to uphold the highest standards of honesty and to deliver on their commitments.

Passion: We expect our people to approach everything with fire in their belly and never give up on doing what they believe is right.

Commitment: Employees who demonstrate perseverance and excellence are richly rewarded. Nothing should be taken lightly as we encourage our people to "work happily and live seriously."

3. PURPOSE
Reasons to exist

To 'make it easy to do business anywhere'.

4. VISION
Aspirations for the future

'We aim to build the future infrastructure of commerce. We envision that our customers will meet, work and live at Alibaba, and that we will be a company that lasts at least 102 years.'

5. STRATEGY
Aligning opportunities, plans and behaviour

- Develop an e-commerce infrastructure that can serve small businesses in China at scale, allowing them to connect with local and international buyers.

Developing an English-language website is crucial to success.

- Create an online payments system that allows customers to receive goods before releasing funds to sellers.
- Raise venture capital funding from company founders and outside investors.
- Focus on succeeding in domestic markets with a view to expand internationally.
- Retain our focus on building a strong team based in China, while attracting talent from overseas to lead our management team.
- Build a loyal customer base through word-of-mouth marketing until we are strongly cash flow positive.
- Streamline operations to keep operating costs to a minimum. (This decision affected things like the numbers of engineers the company employed and the location of its English-language team. One early misstep was the decision to move that team to Silicon Valley. This expensive mistake didn't pay off and was quickly reversed.)
- Expand internationally, form strategic international partnerships and intensify Hong Kong and Indian operations. Market at trade shows in Europe and the U.S.
- Evolve our strategy for countries with low Internet penetration by incorporating online activities with offline operations through local partners.

As we work to get our ideas out into the world and try to find and engage the people those ideas will resonate with, it's easy to fall into the trap of skimming the surface of our story for the facts we believe will give us some tangible advantage. But if we want to give ourselves the best chance of spreading our ideas and creating an impact, we have to get better at telling our real story and living our purpose. We need to invest the time to reflect on why we began on this path and how our past informs our present and future. If we're to do work that matters, we have to dig deeper in order to understand the connection between our personal stories and the work we do. Because now more than ever, our work, not just our job title, is part of our identity.

PART TWO
Building a Story-Driven Company

'Business isn't always about numbers. Actually, it rarely is. It's about people, and emotion. What about the dollars? The cash flow? The share price? Don't kid yourself. Those are the by-products, the results. Anyone who is truly sophisticated about business recognizes this essential truth.'
— *Robert Safian, Editor,* Fast Company

Every business is, by its nature, a catalyst for change. No business can exist without creating a ripple effect by affecting its employees, the place it calls home, the environment around it or the people it serves. We are the creators, engines and supporters of these businesses. The things we stand for or won't stand for are the building blocks of our personal fulfilment and collective prosperity.

Great businesses are forces for good. They design products and services that people need and want. They create jobs that provide people with the dignity of meaningful work. They put food on tables and bring joy to communities. They add value to the economy in more ways than one. They don't just give back. They give by the very virtue of their existence. They can be the making of moments in our days, meaning in our weeks and prosperity in our futures.

Ferguson, Missouri is an unlikely place to open a café selling expensive coffees. The town is now best known for the fatal shooting by a police officer of Michael Brown, an unarmed eighteen-year-old black man. The shooting sparked unrest and riots in Ferguson, whose population is 70 percent black. The local economy suffered on the back of the unrest. Businesses were damaged or destroyed in the riots. The unemployment rate was well above average. The community was left hurting. This is what Howard Schultz witnessed when he stopped off in Ferguson after attending a gathering with Starbucks employees in St Louis, a year after Brown's murder. Here's what his colleague Rodney Hines recalls him saying at the time:

We're absent from this community, and not only are we absent, but we have a responsibility and an opportunity to be here.

Bringing the Starbucks brand to the town was a risk both financially and perceptually. Many people felt there was a disconnect between the brand's offerings and the community's needs. But Starbucks wanted to make a stand and create opportunity. As Fast Company reported, the Ferguson café is just 'one of 15 that Starbucks has committed to opening in underserved communities nationwide by the end of 2018 as part of its larger social-impact agenda'. One of the company's goals is to ensure that every Starbucks employee around the world feels like 'they are part of something bigger than themselves'. And it's working, even in unlikely places like Ferguson.

It's easy to overlook the impact the presence of an employer like Starbucks can have on smaller, less affluent communities if you live in a prosperous urban area where there's a Starbucks on every corner. Starbucks' policy of hiring and training veterans, youth and immigrants is part of the company's wider social-impact agenda. As Starbucks' new CEO Kevin Johnson told Fast Company: 'This is … our reason for being—to leverage our scale for good. It is possible for a publicly traded company to drive an agenda that is not only about shareholder value but is [also] about social impact that helps the people and communities we serve.'

Being story-driven is less about following brand guidelines and more about choosing to act in ways that are consistent with core values. We've all witnessed how a company's purpose and values manifest in the actions of its employees—for good or ill. You have likely experienced an unhelpful doctor's receptionist or a disengaged sales assistant whose behaviour tells you more about the business than their managers realise.

We witnessed a crisis of brand identity played out on the world stage in the spring of 2017, when a passenger was dragged from a United Airlines flight to accommodate crew members who were needed in another city. United's 'Customer Commitment' (the company doesn't seem to have a mission statement) says:

We are committed to providing a level of service to our customers that makes us a leader in the airline industry.

We understand that to do this, we need to have a product we are proud of and employees who like coming to work every day.

When a business strives to be 'the industry leader', the bottom line gets in the way of putting customers first. It's hard to build a product or deliver a service you're proud of when you are focused on winning. The staff involved in the incident seemed unable to deliver on the company's commitment to service. In the aftermath, the CEO's apology started by saying how distressing the incident was for the people who worked for the airline—the customer's ordeal seemed secondary.

> *This is an upsetting event to all of us here at United. I apologize for having to re-accommodate these customers. Our team is moving with a sense of urgency to work with the authorities and conduct our own detailed review of what happened. We are also reaching out to this passenger to talk directly to him and further address and resolve this situation.*
> — *Oscar Munoz, CEO, United Airlines*

He later released a second apology, promising to review policies and procedures—which in every organisation should be consistent with the company's purpose, vision and values. Like Mr Munoz and United, we all need to start there, because every decision we make is dependent on what we prioritise. And every business direction or career path is a series of choices.

Your metric for success is a choice. How you apologise is a choice. The expression you wear as you greet the customer is a choice. Where you source your ingredients is a choice. What you include in or omit from your terms and conditions is a choice. Investment in design. Location. Creating opportunity in low-income communities, prioritising customer care and empowering staff—all choices we're free to make. Rather than feeling overwhelmed about the prospect of getting it wrong, consider these decisions as deliberately placed waymarkers on the road to creating the impact you want to make.

COURAGE AND CONVICTION

Mahatma Ghandi said, 'Happiness is when what you think, what you say, and what you do are in harmony.' Consistently being true to yourself and true to your word is one of the secrets to living a good life. It's also the secret to crafting, telling and living an authentic story that resonates. It sounds simple, but it's hard to do. Sometimes our beliefs, intentions and actions are not in sync—as evidenced by revolving-door diet and exercise plans that begin again every Monday. Our intention and resolve are weakened when we're not fully committed to making values-based decisions. So, we say one thing, yet do another. We bluff and exaggerate instead of seeking clarity through reflection, and then we wonder why we feel like imposters. Authenticity has become an impotent buzzword we casually throw around. Something for all to aspire to. Yet, still the exception, rather than the rule—which is why we are drawn to it when we experience it in the people and places around us.

The leaders we admire and the businesses we respect, support and are loyal to have the courage of their convictions. They're what you might call 'the real deal'. They're not pretending, so they don't have to make it up as they go along. They're simply working hard to be more of who they are—that's why we believe them and believe *in* them. I know that when any one of the team at my local hair salon brings a glass of water, the latest magazines and a hot-drinks menu as soon as I sit down, they're not faking it. Their hospitality and attention to detail are genuine because those values are part of the team's collective identity and they take pride in it.

Marketing should magnify the truth, not manipulate a message. Our job isn't to get everyone to believe us. It's to give the right people something to believe in.

MAXIMUM IMPACT

Every day begins with a quest for more. We're all in pursuit of something—ways to amplify our reach, grow our influence or increase our impact. Any business growth strategy, and even how we personally plan our days, weeks and months, can be plotted on a graph using an x-axis and a y-axis. What every endeavour has in common is time. Time is the constant. This is plotted on the horizontal x-axis. The thing we want to influence, our impact, is represented on the vertical y-axis.

We fail to maximise our impact when we focus on only one or two elements of our story. We achieve maximum impact only when all five elements of our story—backstory, values, purpose, vision, and strategy—are prioritised over time.

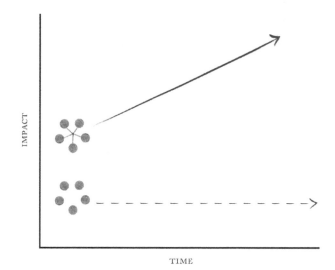

maximum impact

In 2009 the hospitality startup Airbnb was struggling to gain traction, with a total weekly revenue of just $200. The founders needed to do something to increase revenues dramatically if the business was to survive. They could have focused on a strategy for getting more listings and increasing bookings; instead, guided by their purpose and vision, they spent time getting to know their hosts better. One by one they visited hosts in New York (and subsequently other cities) to understand how they could help them to succeed. One of Airbnb's co-founders, Brian Chesky, went one step further and lived entirely in Airbnb properties for several years, describing it as the best way to 'take the pulse' of the company. The Airbnb founders plotted customer success on their y-axis. This deliberate focus on helping hosts was a turning point in the business.

In a digital and globalised world, we have more opportunities and choices than ever before. Sometimes in our attempt to fit in or keep up, we look for the shortcut to success or pursue goals that are more important to others than to ourselves. That's why it's vital to be intentional about prioritising what's on your y-axis. That y-axis is fundamental to shaping your business strategy, culture and identity because it influences your decisions and actions. And you can't experience a sense of fulfilment, even in the face of material success, unless you believe in those choices. It's impossible to be intentional and deliberate if you don't articulate and prioritise what's important to you. You can accidentally build the kind of company or career you want or you can create it on purpose.

THE POWER OF YOUR BACKSTORY
Your company's journey to now

'If you do not know where you come from, then you don't know where you are, and if you don't know where you are, then you don't know where you're going.'
—*Terry Pratchett*, I Shall Wear Midnight

The part of the Nike origin story everyone remembers is the bit where Bill Bowerman, one of the co-founders and a passionate (some might say crazy) athletic coach, poured a synthetic resin into his family's waffle iron one Sunday morning. He had become obsessed with designing a running shoe with a superior grip that would give his athletes an advantage. That battered waffle iron takes pride of place at Nike headquarters. It reminds the people who work there about the company's can-do, scrappy beginnings, and it's symbolic of their purpose—to inspire all athletes. As training manager at Nike, Dennis Reeder says, 'When people understand why we exist, what our foundation is, and who we are today, then they understand that all of our products are still rooted in improving an athlete's performance.' Great companies know how and why they started.

We can't see the hereditary material in our body's cells, but we know it's there. Our DNA may be invisible to the naked eye, but it manifests in the colour of our eyes and the width of our smile. Our genetic makeup not only shapes our physical identity, but can also affect things we can't see, like our long-term health and survival. Similarly, a company's DNA contains the vital information that creates its cultural identity. We may not be able to see intrinsic motivators like purpose and values or the attributes and attitudes that shape them, but they show up in the behaviours of the people who work there. Whether we realise it or not, these intangibles often originate in our backstory.

Understanding your company's backstory is akin to looking directly into your eyes in your reflection in the mirror—not to survey your appearance, attributes or flaws, as we are prone to do, but to begin to recognise who you are. If you've seen a toddler 'discover' himself in a mirror, you'll understand what I mean. It's not until around the age of two that he realises that he is a distinct and separate individual. He is no longer looking at himself—he is looking for himself. He suddenly understands that he and his parents have separate identities—that 'he is'. This epiphany creates a behavioural domino effect. As the child begins to explore who 'me' is, he starts to push and then erect the boundaries that will shape his identity.

Psychologists believe that the ability to distinguish yourself from others is essential to the development of successful social relationships. As business leaders and entrepreneurs, we know that the capacity to truly differentiate one company from others is vital to the success of a brand. Knowing your backstory and its relevance (either as an individual or as a company) enables you to pick up and weave the often loose threads of your past to create an emergent identity in the present. Armed with this narrative and unique identity, you find the direction and meaning that become the scaffold for your brand.

There's a fundamental truth about the importance and value of business backstories that's often overlooked. A company's origin story is much more than a nice-to-have bit of folklore to use as part of a marketing or communications strategy. It's the genesis of the company's values and purpose—the foundation upon which everything else is built. The awareness of the particular circumstances and events that made us who we are grounds and grows us, as individuals, companies and societies.

Consider how the backstory of the outdoor-wear company Patagonia has shaped the company's purpose, vision and strategy for four decades. Patagonia was founded by a group of surfers and climbers who cared deeply about the environment. Their backstory influences day-to-day business decisions. Every part of Patagonia's business strategy must support their purpose, which is to 'Build the best product, cause no unnecessary harm, [and] use business to inspire and implement solutions to the environmental crisis'. The company's identity affects its operations, culture and ultimately its legacy. That alignment of strategy and values played out in a very practical way during the Black Friday marketing frenzy in 2011, when Patagonia launched the 'Don't Buy This Jacket' campaign in *The New York Times*.

Here's part of the message the company communicated to customers in that advert:

Because Patagonia wants to be in business for a good long time—and leave a world inhabitable for our kids—we want to do the opposite of every other business today. We ask you to buy less and to reflect before you spend a dime on this jacket or anything else.

Starbucks founder Howard Schultz grew up in a poor New York neighbourhood. He tells the powerful story of his father—a delivery man with no health insurance, who broke his leg and subsequently lost his job. Schultz wanted to build Starbucks in a way that would make his dad proud. 'Health insurance was the first thing we did, which was in honor of my father.' The offer of comprehensive and affordable health coverage to employees and their families has been 'a cornerstone' of Starbucks' 'partner-focused' culture for more than two decades. The company pays 70 percent of the premium and 100 percent of preventative care services.

Our stories are potent drivers of our deepest motivations and biggest dreams. Owning those stories helps us to make sense of our place in the world and of our potential to change it.

THE IMPORTANCE OF VALUES
Your company's guiding values

'It's not hard to make decisions when you know what your values are.'
—*Roy Disney*

Values are part of our personal and organisational GPS, constantly indicating our next move. Our sense of right and wrong enables us to function as individuals and flourish as a society.

When our values and behaviours are in sync, we experience a sense of equilibrium, and when they're not, we feel disappointed and dissatisfied. We like to believe that our decisions are made using rational judgement, through careful assembly and assessment of the relevant facts. But our decision-making process is more complex and far less rational than we realise. We make decisions with our heads and our hearts. Our instincts and biases come into play, causing us to do things we may later regret or that are not always in our best interests.

We subconsciously make values-based decisions all the time, but when we clearly articulate our values, we create a kind of moral shorthand that helps us to consciously and consistently act with integrity. This is especially important in groups, like companies, when people with different backgrounds, life experiences and worldviews come together to work towards a common goal. How do we decide on the best course of action when everyone brings their individual opinions and biases to the table? In a group dynamic, we need to create an agreed-upon and shared worldview, a set of guiding beliefs through which our decisions can be filtered. This enables us to make good judgement calls even in stressful situations. Shared values allow us to unite around shared ideals. When we agree upon them, we are also agreeing to be bound by the behaviours that support the upholding of them. In organisations, this encourages both responsibility and accountability. An organisation's culture is a manifestation of its values.

The benefits of a strong, values-led company culture are best illustrated by the online shoe retailer Zappos. It was founded in 1999 by Nick Swinmurn and Tony Hsieh, and acquired by Amazon in 2009 for a reported $1.2 billion. As CEO, Hsieh was the driver of Zappos' extraordinary company culture. The company became the poster child for building a values-driven business. Zappos' core values and the foundation of their extraordinary culture are published on the company website:

Our 10 Core Values

1. *Deliver WOW through service.*
2. *Embrace and drive change.*
3. *Create fun and a little weirdness.*
4. *Be adventurous, creative, and open-minded.*
5. *Pursue growth and learning.*
6. *Build open and honest relationships with communication.*
7. *Build a positive team and family spirit.*
8. *Do more with less.*
9. *Be passionate and determined.*
10. *Be humble.*

These values are not just filling whitespace on the website's About page—they are lived in every decision the management and employees make every day. Because Zappos aspires to deliver incredible service, it adopts a customer-centric strategy. Call centre employees don't have sales scripts, and there are no limits on the duration of customer support calls—as evidenced by the record-breaking longest customer service call on April 4, 2017, by Stephanie V., who was on the phone with a customer for 10 hours and 51 minutes. Zappos employees are not instructed to follow the rules; they are encouraged to live their values and do the right thing.

The next time you experience bad service, take a look around you for clues about the values the employees in that business are being encouraged to uphold. When the doctor's receptionist ignores your arrival, and continues tapping away on her computer while chatting to her colleagues from behind an unwelcoming counter, you sense she's been taught to prioritise efficiency. When the beauty therapist pushes you to buy an expensive aftercare product that you don't need so she can hit her monthly commission target, you have an inkling about what outcomes she's been trained to achieve. When a company's call centre answers your call according to what an algorithm tells them about how valuable a customer you are, and not according to the time you called, it's an indication of their beliefs about what's right and fair. It might be possible to hide behind excuses for a while, but actions really do speak louder than words.

THE VALUE OF PURPOSE
Your reason to exist

'People work better when they know what the goal is and why.'
—Elon Musk

What's wrong with simply making and marketing things purely for profit? Surely that's what sustains free-market economies. Isn't that what capitalism is about? Why do we need to care about the relevance of our work or the reason our company exists? We need to care because even in a digital world, human capital is the backbone of thriving economies, and humans are intrinsically motivated and have innate psychological needs. Unlike some lower-order mammals, we often do things for their own sake, not simply in a bid to survive and reproduce or for material gain.

The Theory of Self-Determination explains that human nature exhibits the inherent growth tendencies of effort, agency and commitment. We are driven by our innate psychological need for competence, relatedness and autonomy. We are hardwired to fulfil our potential. We choose to do things that don't directly or materially benefit us because it feels good to do them and because doing them contributes to our wellbeing. We are our best selves when we have a sense of control over our destiny and feel supported by our community to achieve mastery. We flourish when we do work we're proud of and are nurtured in a supportive social environment. As we learned earlier in the book, researchers like Dan Ariely have shown that we need to feel that we're making a contribution to something that's bigger than ourselves. Without a sense of purpose, our health and wellbeing suffer.

Research by Gallup estimates that more than two-thirds of U.S. employees feel disengaged from their work. Disengagement costs between $450 billion and $550 billion in lost productivity per year. It turns out that employee engagement and business performance go hand-in-hand; companies with more-engaged employees experience higher levels of customer satisfaction and are more profitable. Employees don't only want their workplaces to pay them fairly or to meet their basic needs for a safe working environment, contracted hours and paid annual leave—though these things are vital. They also want to have a sense of autonomy and purpose and feel like they are stakeholders in the company's future. Successful businesses are powered by people who feel fulfilled. Having a strong sense of purpose is good for people, and it's good for business, too.

We each have a responsibility to create, and a hand in creating, a future for the next generation. The daily activities of a business have a huge impact on the wellbeing of people and the planet. It's important to have a corporate social responsibility policy and crucial to understand the wider contribution your business will make to society. Rather than simply advocating for limiting the damage we do to the world, we can proactively engage in having a positive impact. We can set an intention to change our tiny corner of the world.

As we know, customers, users and donors increasingly want to support businesses that share their values. That's especially true of millennials, the largest consumer demographic in the U.S. Research undertaken at the University of Southern California found that 87 percent of millennials base their purchasing decisions on companies' corporate and social responsibility policies. Today's customers want to know that you care about more than just making money. If you don't understand why your business exists beyond to turn a profit, or if you're not communicating your purpose, then you're making it harder for people to get behind you. When you know what you stand for, you have absolute clarity about the reason you're the best choice for the people you want to serve—and so do they.

We only have to revisit the 2016 U.S. Presidential election to underscore why it's vital to be clear about your purpose. Political commentators like *The Australian's* Janet Albrechtsen, still puzzled about what happened and why Hillary Clinton lost the election, have reported on the perspective of authors Jonathan Allen and Amie Parnes in their book, *Shattered: Inside Hillary Clinton's Doomed Campaign.*

> *The authors draw on a treasure trove of insights. None more so than Clinton's failure to find a message. The candidate who eschewed unscripted interactions with voters gave speeches that failed to connect her to a cause larger than herself. Clinton couldn't explain with power or emotion why, after a quarter of a century in politics, she wanted to be president. What would she do for Americans?*

What's even more important than the opinions and commentary, though, is how Clinton explains her shortcomings in her best-selling book, *What Happened.* 'In politics, the personal narrative is vital,' she says.

But my story—or at least how I've always told it—was never the kind of narrative that made everyone sit up and take notice. We yearn for that showstopping tale— that one-sentence pitch that captures something magical about America; that hooks you and won't let you go. Mine wasn't it.

Yet there is another story of my life; one that I believe is as inspiring as any other. I wish I had claimed it and told it more proudly.

Almost a year after her election defeat, Clinton is sitting on a sofa in London, chatting with Irish comedian and talk show host Graham Norton about her new book and the circumstances that surrounded her defeat. She is wearing a yellow jacket, black pants and an orthopaedic boot to protect her recently fractured toe. The layers of political armour begin to melt away, and shoots of her vulnerability and humanity poke through. She is not trying to make a statement or an impression. She is transparent, funny and relatable. She is finally claiming her story. It's as if we are seeing her for the very first time.

Clinton talks about a moment at one of the debates during the closing weeks of the election campaign: the time her opponent, Donald Trump, positioned himself directly behind her, 'looming', close enough for her to feel his presence. It felt like he was trying to intimidate and unnerve her—to put her off or make her lose her composure. She recounts the moment with regret, giving us some insight into what she was thinking at the time. What she really wanted to do was turn around and tell Trump to back off, but she didn't because she was afraid of how her actions would be interpreted. In that moment, she felt she needed to do the thing that was expected—not what was true to her.

Now, as the former First Lady, Senator and Secretary of State of the United States, and the most qualified candidate ever to run for office, her answers to Norton's questions are peppered by insights into the news stories and criticism she had been paying attention to all her life. The things that came between who she was and who she wanted to be. Commentary about her marriage and her health, opinions about her appearance and the shrillness of her voice—all clearly noted and taken on board in an attempt to adopt the persona of the leader she thought people wanted. As the interview is coming to a close, Hillary talks about her mission to make women understand that they have a voice— her focus now no longer on winning, but on the contribution she might make going forward.

Even if on paper you are the most qualified, even if you can demonstrate that your product is superior, even if you have a watertight rationale to demonstrate that you are the best choice by a mile, people will be reluctant to support you unless they believe you. And they won't believe you unless they can see you. People need to understand what you stand for, just as much as they need to know how your policies, products and services can help them. You need to give them a reason to be loyal to your brand, rather than a hundred reasons why you're better than the competition. There is no back door to the affinity we all crave with our audience. No amount of attention you can buy will get you to this point. Loyalty is achieved only with resonance.

VISION
Your aspiration for the future

'To begin with the end in mind means to start with a clear understanding of your destination. It means to know where you're going so that you better understand where you are now and so that the steps you take are always in the right direction.'
—*Stephen Covey,* The 7 Habits of Highly Effective People

Without a purpose, we don't know why we're on the journey. But without a vision, we don't know the destination.

The terms "mission" and "vision" are often confused and used interchangeably in organisations, so it's worth making the distinction here. Your mission is your purpose—which is the term I prefer and have chosen to use for the sake of clarity. As we've explored in the previous section, it's the reason your company exists. Your purpose is why you do what you do today and every day. Your vision is your aspiration for the future—the contribution you or your work will make.

In recent times, we've witnessed the phenomenal success of the business application Slack. I believe the company's clear vision—to build 'the ecosystem for work'—has played a big part in that success. Slack is a cloud-based collaboration platform that connects teams with tools, services, and resources that improve communication and productivity. The company name is an acronym for 'Searchable Log of All Conversation and Knowledge'—which I didn't know until I began my research for this book. Slack is also the fastest-growing business application in history. Its rapid adoption and popularity are thought to be due to the widespread perception that email overload is diminishing productivity in organisations of all sizes.

Slack's founder, Stewart Butterfield, wrote an insightful post on Medium in 2014, the bones of which had been an earlier internal memo to his team, explaining his vision for the company and how he believed they would succeed. In his mind, they were not simply selling a chat service or a communication platform—they were selling organisational transformation in various forms. As he wrote,

> ...if we are selling "a reduction in the cost of communication" or "zero effort knowledge management" or "making better decisions, faster" or "all your team communication, instantly searchable, available wherever you go" or "75% less email" or some other valuable result of adopting Slack, we will find many more buyers.

It would have been easy to get bogged down in the minutiae of feature development. Instead, Stewart painted a picture of the future for his team. He didn't simply invite them to make a better product; he inspired them to do work they were proud to have done. The clearly stated shared vision enabled the team to move forward with a coherent strategy. At the time of this writing, Slack has 9 million weekly active users in a hundred countries. Seventy-seven percent of the *Fortune* 100 companies use the application. The company has gone from zero to a $5 billion valuation in four years.

How many of us (or those who work with us) could articulate our vision for the future of our company with such clarity and conviction? It's not easy to measure the impact of having a clear purpose and vision—which is why deliberately designing a business around them is often overlooked. And yet, when we dig deeper, we find that beloved brands, the ones that are successful by every measure, do exactly that. Your brand's story has the power to be a map, mirror and magnet, and your vision keeps you on track, enabling you to attract like-minded people who want to create the future with you.

STRATEGY
The alignment of opportunities, plans and behaviour

'If you don't know where you're going, any road will take you there.'
—George Harrison

If a vision is a distant goal in the future, the strategy is the route to getting there—the plan for realising your vision. Often, we start with an idea for a product or service, unsure of the contribution the product or business will make over time. We become so focused on succeeding in the present that we forget to take a longer-term term view of our potential to create an impact. By only planning to achieve near-term goals, we're in danger of going down blind alleys in an attempt to be competitive or getting distracted and doing things that don't serve us in the long run. It can be more helpful to use our vision as a jumping-off point for our strategy and work backwards, creating the plan that will get us there. The vision informs the strategy.

Think of your strategy as a path of stepping stones that you navigate to your goal. Your plan, chunked down into manageable pieces. Having a strategy enables you to ask better tactical questions. How will you achieve your vision? What should you prioritise? Where do you need to allocate resources? What skills do you have? What capabilities do you need to build? What comes first and why? Strategy is the how. Let's look at some practical examples in action.

Howard Schultz's vision for Starbucks to become 'the third place' meant that he and his team had to consider more than just the quality of the coffee beans. Every part of the experience, from seating to music, lighting to product naming architecture, was taken into account. The 'third place' vision influenced everything from café locations to staff training. Likewise, when Jack Ma envisaged creating opportunities for Chinese entrepreneurs, he understood that this would involve building a trusted digital payment infrastructure (Alipay) that anyone could use. And as we've seen earlier in the book, Elon Musk's first 'Secret Master Plan', published in August 2006, breaks down exactly how his company will start accelerating the world's switch to sustainable energy:

Build sports car
Use that money to build an affordable car
Use that money to build an even more affordable car
While doing above, also provide zero emission electric power generation options

This four-point strategy was created by working backwards from his sustainable-energy vision. Musk believed that an electric car without compromises was critical to expediting 'the move from a mine-and-burn hydrocarbon economy towards a solar electric economy'.

Business building is not necessarily linear, but it is a progression. Important first and next steps on any business- or career-building journey are born from understanding what we are working towards. Without that clarity, we can end up walking around in ever-decreasing circles, getting nowhere.

CASE STORIES

'A business that makes nothing but money is a poor kind of business.'
—*Henry Ford*

It's often easier to understand how something works in practice by seeing examples of how others have done it. That's why I've curated case studies, using the Story-Driven Framework, from a variety of businesses for you. Some are global, publicly traded companies you will have heard of; some are small businesses you have never come across. The variety of businesses illustrated shows that the framework works whether you write code, fill teeth or pour coffee shots for a living. We're starting with Tesla because it's such an important and elegant example that it's worth revisiting in its entirety. But you'll find other, less-well-known examples here, too.

First, a note about the case stories. The company stories I'm sharing here were gathered either by speaking directly to the business owners or by doing a ton of research into the founder's and company's origin, history, progress and growth. Where it was possible, with purpose and vision statements,

I've quoted directly from company documentation or other published material. Things get harder when it comes to the individual company strategies, especially if I've been unable to interview the founder or team. So, in some cases the strategy I've laid out comes from retracing the company's steps to today, rather than from something the company has publicly documented. These case stories serve as a guide only and are not meant to represent the facts about an entire corporate strategy or to imply a company's endorsement of the Story-Driven Framework.

TESLA

BACKSTORY
Journey to now

Tesla, Inc., was founded in 2003 by engineers Martin Eberhard and Marc Tarpenning, who believed it was possible to create an electric car without compromises. Industrialist and entrepreneur Elon Musk's involvement in the company began when he led the Series A investment round in 2004. Far from being just an investor in the company, Musk is credited with being the architect of Tesla's success.

Elon Musk was born and raised in Pretoria, South Africa. His ancestors hailed from Canada and America. His maternal grandfather, Joshua N. Haldeman, was a chiropractor with a passion for aviation and exploration. Haldeman moved his family, their Cadillac and his single-engine airplane from Saskatchewan to South Africa in 1950 in search of adventure. In 1954, he and his wife, Winnifred, flew 30,000 miles from South Africa to Australia and back in their tiny plane. Musk's grandfather left his mother, Maye, and her siblings with the impression that they were capable of anything.

The young Elon Musk was an inquisitive introvert. According to his mother, 'he seemed to understand things quicker than other kids'. He had a tough childhood, though; his father was strict, his parents divorced and he struggled to fit in with his peers. He was seen as a know-it-all and was bullied at school. When the school day finished, Musk headed to the local bookstore and stayed there reading for hours until it closed. His brother Kimbal says it was not unusual for him 'to read ten hours a day'. He ran out of books to read in both the school library and his local library, so he started to read the Encyclopaedia Britannica.

Musk became interested in computers when he was ten, and he programmed a space-themed computer game called Blastar when he was twelve. He sold the source code to a magazine for $500.

As a teenager, Musk was influenced by Douglas Adams' book The Hitchhiker's Guide to the Galaxy. He learned that 'one of the really tough things is figuring out what questions to ask,' but 'once you figure out the question, then the answer is relatively easy.' His question became, What things will have a great impact on the future of humanity's destiny?

He emigrated to Canada when he was seventeen and went on to study engineering at the University of Pennsylvania. Musk is a serial entrepreneur; he founded the successful Internet and technology companies X.com (which later merged with Confinity and became PayPal) and

SpaceX (a private aerospace company) before investing in and leading Tesla.

When he invested in Tesla, he was backing a vision he had believed in long before he met the Tesla founders. Years earlier, Musk had been about to embark on a PhD program at Stanford University to study sustainable batteries, but he dropped out to start an Internet company during the dotcom boom in the late '90s. He became Tesla CEO in 2008 and he plays a hands-on role in the company, overseeing engineering, development and design.

Musk's biographer Ashlee Vance sums up Musk's vision this way:

He is less a CEO chasing riches than a general marshaling troops to secure victory. Where Mark Zuckerberg wants to help you share baby photos, Musk wants to ... well ... save the human race from self-imposed or accidental annihilation.

The possible source of Musk's drive and vision? As Musk told Vance:

Maybe I read too many comics as a kid. In the comics, it always seems like they are trying to save the world. It seems like one should try to make the world a better place because the inverse makes no sense.

VALUES
Guiding beliefs

- Being useful
- Curiosity
- Determination
- Imagination
- Boldness
- Community

PURPOSE
Reason to exist

To accelerate 'the advent of sustainable energy, so that we can imagine far into the future and life is still good'.

VISION
Aspiration for the future

'Expedite the move from a mine-and-burn hydrocarbon economy towards a solar electric economy'.

STRATEGY
Aligning opportunities, plans and behaviour

- Bring compelling, affordable electric cars to market.
- 'Create stunning solar roofs with seamlessly integrated battery storage'.
- 'Expand the electric vehicle product line to address all major segments'.
- 'Develop a self-driving capability that is 10X safer than manual via massive fleet learning'.

- 'Enable your car to make money for you when you aren't using it'.

PRESENT AND FUTURE

In 2017, Tesla was Consumer Reports' top-ranked car brand in the U.S. and eighth in the world. At the time of this writing, it has a higher valuation than the two U.S. auto-making giants GM and Ford. But just as important for the people who build and drive them, Tesla vehicles are preventing billions of tons of carbon dioxide emissions from entering the earth's atmosphere. Pre-orders of Tesla's mass-market Model 3 vehicle have reached almost half a million, and an average of 1800 new orders are placed every day. The next stage in the advancement of the company's mission 'to accelerate the advent of sustainable energy' and have a real impact on climate change is to launch an electric semi-truck in 2019.

EMMA BRIDGEWATER POTTERY

BACKSTORY
Journey to now

Emma had imagined herself following in her father's footsteps, working for a publisher in a tiny office in London's SoHo district. She started getting her ducks in a row by graduating with an English degree, but her career plans took a turn when she chose to follow her mother's spirit instead. Emma was out shopping for the perfect gift for her mother's birthday—a pair of mismatched cups and saucers that could live on her kitchen dresser, a gift that would remind her that even though speaking was difficult today, because of her brain injury, she and Emma would sit down and have a chat over a cup of tea one day soon. Everything Emma found in the shops was either 'too formal or too clunky'. And so, armed with some sketches and without any formal design training, Emma headed north to Stoke-on-Trent to find a potter to make her designs.

Emma had a joyful, bohemian childhood, growing up in what we would today call a blended family of loving parents, stepparents and siblings. Her mother was a huge influence on her, the person who always brought joy to every experience. Emma's earliest memories are of family trips to the coast, of setting the table with mismatched crockery for dinner parties, hanging fairy lights from apple trees and putting on her old bridesmaid's dress before the guests arrived. Whatever home the family lived in, it always had a kitchen dresser laden with her mother's treasures.

Post-university, with thoughts of a career in publishing abandoned, Emma worked in New York for two successful female entrepreneurs who designed and made knitwear. Their company, Muir & Osborne, sold garments to high-end retailers; it was creative and fun. You've likely seen one of their most famous creations—the red sweater with sheep on the front that Lady Diana Spencer wore when her engagement to Prince Charles was announced. Emma's experience at Muir & Osbourne would help her later to structure her business.

The seeds of her future business empire were sown when Emma was shopping for the perfect birthday gift for her mum. She searched high and low for 'the perfect, beautiful thing, that said how much she loved her'. Emma was searching for two cups and saucers that would say 'we want to be together'. Nothing in the china shop felt right. 'It just hit [her] there and then, [she'd] have to make those cups and saucers [herself].' Emma wanted to make 'the kind of colourful, friendly, warm, mismatched pottery ... which was what [her mother's] kitchen was full of.' Her intention from the start was to design and manufacture pottery that people would fall in love with. Emma didn't want to make the cheapest mug; she wanted to make 'the loveliest mug'.

Emma's childhood memories of family gatherings around the table have influenced how her company's products are designed and made to this day. She says, 'There is something of the altar about the kitchen table. There's something almost sacred about the cups and the teapots and the plates—the things you use every day.'

Emma Bridgewater Pottery began production in 1985 in Stoke-on-Trent, the home of England's pottery industry. Emma (who was just twenty-three at the time) says 'she arrived just as everyone else was leaving'. She was saddened to witness firsthand that the traditional pottery industry was dying. It's estimated that the area had up to 4,000 bottle kilns in the 1800s, but by the time Emma Bridgewater launched, the local industry was in decline. Companies like Wedgewood and Royal Doulton were shutting up shop or outsourcing production to China. Factory closures meant that many skilled craftsmen were unemployed.

Not long after she started her business, Emma met her future husband, furniture designer Matthew Rice, at a design trade fair, and they now run Emma Bridgewater together. Today their company makes 25,000 pieces of hand-decorated pottery per week and employs 250 people. Emma still remembers her first scouting trip to the area and the feeling of wanting to resurrect one of the abandoned factories. She would love to increase the number of employees to 2,500 one day. Creating jobs is the 'greatest privilege I can imagine', she says.

> *For me the driving thing is—it was at the beginning when I was thinking about mum's kitchen and it still is now. It is every time I'm designing. Those meals where everyone is going to get together, the family is all arriving on a Friday night. The talking and laughing and drinking and sitting up all night—that feeling of connection and love. I really believe that the pottery can hold that.*

VALUES
Guiding beliefs

- Joy
- Family
- Tradition
- Passion
- Community
- Practicality

PURPOSE
Reason to exist

'To make things that make everyday life a little bit nicer'.

VISION
Aspiration for the future

To keep the British manufacturing tradition alive.

STRATEGY
Aligning opportunities, plans and behaviour

- Create a practical everyday product that's pretty enough to display in the kitchen dresser and functional enough to be used and enjoyed every day.
- Design products 'that are beautiful to look at but also a pleasure to use'.
- Create products that are handmade and decorated in England.
- Position and price products at the higher end of the market.
- Use multiple sales channels: bricks-and-mortar retailers, resellers and direct to the consumer online and in the factory shop.
- Offer customers membership in a Lifetime Collectors Club, with membership discounts and early access to sales and news.
- Form licensing partnerships with like-minded companies such as Liberty.

PRESENT AND FUTURE

In 2016 Emma Bridgewater's annual revenue was a reported £15 million. The company plans to increase production by 40 percent by 2019. It is still independently owned and operated because Emma believes that family-owned businesses are good not just for owners, but also for employees and the economy. 'You're thinking about a ten-year horizon and the economy needs that stability—we all need that stability, that sanity.'

MISS GERTRUDE SALON

BACKSTORY
Journey to now

You have to know where Miss Gertrude's hair salon is to find it—tucked away off one of the hip main streets in Melbourne's creative hub, Fitzroy. Even when you arrive at the address, you're still not quite sure you're in the right place. The entire working area of the salon is hidden from the street. The location and salon layout are clues as to what you'll find beyond the entrance. This unpretentious salon is staffed entirely by introverts. The atmosphere is calm and inviting. As you enter, it almost feels like you're in an upmarket, airy café, complete with barista coffee and tea served in Japanese teapots with Ginger Thin biscuits. This successful salon does no paid marketing. What brings clients here is word of mouth about the great stylists and unique atmosphere.

Leanne Spence, one of the owners, who is also salon manager and creative director, grew up in a working-class suburb of Glasgow where there was high unemployment. She came from a very loving, supportive family but was painfully shy as a child and would always be found playing alone with glitter and paint. She loved making things, watching nature documentaries and reading books under her bedcovers with a torch late into the night. While Leanne was close to her family, she also felt different from them. She dreamt of travelling to the places she'd seen on the Lonely Planet shows.

Her school was far from an inspiring place. In an era of high unemployment, teachers seemed demotivated and students didn't have much to aspire to. Leanne knew she wanted to do something creative when she left school, but the options seemed limited at a time when many of her friends ended up unemployed and on the dole once they'd left school. You were lucky to have a job at all during the recession of the early '90s in Scotland. When she was just fifteen, with a lot of encouragement from her parents to give it a go, Leanne applied for a hairdressing apprenticeship at the prestigious Rainbow Room International salon. She was so terrified she spent the night before the interview and the journey there in her mother's car in tears and still has no idea how she was accepted. 'The way my family talked about me having an apprenticeship and becoming a hairdresser was as if I had become a brain surgeon.'

Despite 'falling into' a career in hairdressing and being painfully shy, she excelled as a stylist in an extrovert's world. Leanne became director's assistant and won the Apprentice of the Year and Best Young Graduate awards. She started to experiment with clothes and crazy hair colours. She went out to clubs with the other stylists and tried to be more like them. Her introversion felt like a fatal flaw and it took her many years to realise and accept that it's just who she is.

Hairdressing gave Leanne the opportunity to fulfil her dream to travel, which she did for a year on cruise ships. When she landed in Melbourne, she planted her flag.

Leanne worked in and then managed a salon and helped to establish a new one—Miss Gertrude. She felt totally out of her depth but recognised that despite feeling like this on many occasions throughout her life, she always managed to do the things she put her mind to. The owners gave her the freedom to make Miss Gertrude her own. Leanne's intention was to create her own unique brand of salon experience, devoid of the ego-driven stylist. In the salon's second year of business and after a ton of hard work, she bought out one of the partners and became co-owner of the salon she had purposefully built.

In an industry that is typically flamboyant, Miss Gertrude exudes quiet confidence. The stylists don't enter industry competitions or train to compete for awards. Their focus is on delighting their clients and solving their problems with creative styles and environmentally friendly products rather than on upselling hair care products clients don't need. What's immediately obvious is the teamwork. Everyone, regardless of seniority, pulls their weight. There is no task too lowly for anyone, and there's no superstar status, just pride in a job well done. In an industry that's known for burnout and hard work for poor pay, Leanne has created a culture where her team feel empowered and valued. They each have a sense of their contribution to the team, the prosperity of the business and the wellbeing of their local creative community. They are encouraged to be themselves and bring their ideas to work every day. Leanne says:

> *Our staff all have different interests apart from*
> *hair. One is a potter, another is a horticulture tissue*
> *culture specialist. They just have a common interest in*

hairdressing and are all genuine people, which is why the salon is so unique.

VALUES
Guiding beliefs

- Creativity
- Respect for individuality
- Teamwork
- People and community first
- Collaboration
- Fulfilment
- The little things

PURPOSE
Reason to exist

To be everything our clients and stylists want from a hair salon.

VISION
Aspiration for the future

We want to be an asset to our creative community, providing meaningful employment to the people who are part of our team and the best experience our clients have ever had.

STRATEGY
Aligning opportunities, plans and behaviour

- Use values-based leadership and training to create a strong customer service culture.

- Hold weekly staff meetings to keep the team updated, iron out challenges and celebrate progress.

- Provide outstanding customer care.

- Use only environmentally friendly, Australian products.

- Provide an in-salon café and drinks menu.

- Use our training to improve our skills and service, not to compete in industry competitions.

- Build a referral-based business.

- Use no paid marketing; rely only on word-of-mouth marketing.

- Aim for controlled growth, not expansion or diversification.

- Send key team members overseas for education and training.

- Train new stylists according to best practices, international trends and our unique culture.

- Hire for cultural fit.

PRESENT AND FUTURE

Miss Gertrude has garnered 2,000-plus positive reviews on MyLocalSalon.com in only six years. The management have no plans for expansion. They continue to thrive by doing what they do well.

WIKIPEDIA

BACKSTORY
Journey to now

Doris Ann Wales ran a tiny, one-room schoolhouse in Alabama, alongside her mother, Erma Dudley. Naturally, Doris's four children became pupils. When Doris's son Jimmy was three years old, she bought a World Book Encyclopaedia from a door-to-door salesman. Jimmy would spend hours reading the entries, then updating them with the stickers that were mailed out by the publisher when an article was out of date. He transferred schools after eighth grade to prepare for university, graduated with a finance degree when he was twenty years old, and later earned a master's degree in finance.

It was while he was playing fantasy games at university that his interest in the Internet was sparked. Wales wrote computer code in his free time and worked in financial trading during the day. In 1996, he decided to leave his job to become an Internet entrepreneur, developing what he calls a 'guy-oriented search engine', which didn't make much money but provided enough capital for Wales to create a free online encyclopaedia, written by expert volunteers. Nupedia, as it was called, failed because of the extensive review process. The top-down academic structure was demotivating for contributors and the review process was so slow that it killed the project.

In 2001, Nupedia's editor, Larry Sanger, was introduced to the concept of a wiki, which would transform the submission and editing process. It was Sanger who dubbed the new project Wikipedia. The project went live on the new domain five days after it was created, on 15th January 2001. By 2015, the site had 18 billion page views per month.

VALUES
Guiding beliefs

- Openness
- Collaboration
- Community
- Neutrality
- Respect
- Improvements over rules

PURPOSE
Reason to exist

'To benefit readers by acting as an encyclopaedia, a comprehensive written compendium that contains information on all branches of knowledge…'.

VISION
Aspiration for the future

'Imagine a world in which every single person on the planet is given free access to the sum of all human knowledge.'

STRATEGY
Aligning opportunities, plans and behaviour

- Maintain a free service for all users.
- Operate as a non-profit organisation in order to serve users.

- Be open access for all users.
- Use volunteer contributors (in addition to the Wikimedia Foundation's paid staff).
- Follow a mediation process when disputes arise.
- Never accept paid advertising.
- Focus on knowledge as a service and build infrastructure that supports this goal.
- Build strong, diverse communities that encourage access to free knowledge.

PRESENT AND FUTURE

At the time of writing in late 2017, Wikipedia has 5.5 million articles and is available in 299 languages. It is the world's fifth-most-visited website with a worldwide monthly readership of 495 million.

LES MILLS GROUP

BACKSTORY
Journey to now

Philip Mills choreographed his first barbell workout in the remote city of Auckland, New Zealand in 1990. Today he is the CEO of Les Mills International, the hugely successful global fitness brand.

The Les Mills Group is named after Philip's father, Les, an Olympic athlete who represented New Zealand four times in track and field events. He won a gold medal for discus in the 1966 Commonwealth Games. You could say sport and fitness are in the family's blood, as Les's wife, Colleen, daughter Donna and son Philip (the company's CEO) were all national athletes.

Les opened his first gym in Auckland in 1968. Philip joined his father in the business in 1980 and began to look for innovative ways to motivate people. The company was one of the pioneers of group fitness classes and aerobic programs set to music. Les Mills' hugely successful barbell program, now named BODYPUMP, was introduced in 1990, and other programs followed, including an on-demand online fitness program. The company also has an instructor certification program and partners with Reebok to design a range of specialised fitness clothing and equipment.

VALUES
Guiding beliefs

One tribe: 'We are family. A family company united in our love of movement, music and the pursuit of healthy living for ourselves and our planet.'

Be brave: 'We push hard to always do our best work; everyone around us here is in the relentless pursuit of improvement.'

Change the world: 'Changing the world won't be easy. There'll be doubters, haters. Those who cling tight to yesterday's ideas. But here, in this place, and wherever the tribe is gathered, we dare to dream.'

'Let's create new and better ways to help people to take their first steps on the road to fitness ... [and] create life-changing fitness experiences every time.'

PURPOSE
Reason to exist

'To create a fitter, healthier planet'.

VISION
Aspiration for the future

'Transform the global health system, by preventing major health issues caused by inactivity and obesity'.

STRATEGY
Aligning opportunities, plans and behaviour

- Develop group fitness routines that people love.
- Create an instructor certification program.
- Train a network of instructors.
- Use cutting-edge research and science to create an effective and immersive experience.
- Create new workouts every three months.
- Enable 20 million workouts in live venues by 2020.
- Target 100 million people a week having a Les Mills experience.
- Broaden our reach with club coaching.
- Advance into new territories.

PRESENT AND FUTURE

One hundred thirty thousand Les Mills instructors deliver classes to more than 6 million people every week, in more than 100 countries around the world. To put that into perspective, the population of New Zealand today stands at 4.5 million.

SAME DAY DENTAL

BACKSTORY
Journey to now

Charles Cole wanted to be a dentist from the time he was nine years old. He's not exactly sure why, and even then he recognised that it was a weird aspiration for a little kid to have. But buoyed by his ambition, he worked hard at school and went to college to realise his dream.

In the late '70s, he became an associate in a dental practice and set about trying to make a difference to patients by improving their care. Dr Cole wanted to help the practice to computerise so dentists could spend more time with patients, instead of being bogged down in insurance claims and paperwork. But his colleagues didn't share his enthusiasm for change. After eighteen months, he realized that if he wanted to create meaningful change for patients, he'd have to go out on his own and practice dentistry his way.

Aged just twenty-six, Dr Cole invested in his first established dental office. While he had a clear sense of how he wanted to treat patients, he knew nothing about business. Conventional wisdom and the business model in the dental industry at the time, and still to a large extent today, rewarded productivity, with a direct correlation between the number of patients and revenue. At the time, dentists aspired to build the $100,000 practice—that was the marker of success.

His practice was viable, but Dr Cole was burned out and unhappy. He felt under pressure to maintain the existing culture of the office to ensure that the business remained profitable. His dental school education hadn't equipped him with the skills to be successful at building patient relationships, and showing vulnerability was deemed unprofessional and risky. His predecessors, who were divorced and chain smokers, were his only role models and he thought that if he was to avoid failure, he needed to emulate them. They must know a thing or two—after all, they were successful, right? Dr Cole felt empty and inauthentic, but was too insecure to trust that being true to himself would be enough.

His two biggest fears were losing patients and being himself. He built up the practice and then sold it, repeating this process of buying and growing an established practice twice, moving to Alaska and then back to Michigan in search of fulfilment. Each time, Dr Cole used the same formula to build a successful practice. He doubled or tripled the business in pursuit of cash flow and security. But he wasn't being true to himself.

In the '90s, he dabbled in patient record software, but he was just a little too early to the game. In 2001, Dr Cole opened his third office, falling into the trap of doing the same thing and expecting a different result. Now the goalposts had shifted and the marker of success was the million-dollar practice. In 2007, he invested in a machine that would allow him to make crowns in a day. This would be a turning point in his thinking about what was possible in a practice that sought to give patients what they wanted. After his kids graduated, he moved back to Alaska to work part-time in another dental practice. In December 2012, at the age of fifty-nine, he was let go without warning. Dr Cole had no backup plan and not enough of a nest egg to retire. After thirty-five years in practice, he decided to start afresh and build his very first dental office from scratch. He refused to buy an existing practice. This time it would be different.

Dr Cole wanted to create a truly patient-centric practice, one that would treat and solve their dental problems on the same day. A practice that would not force the patient into the office's ideal schedule, but would be about service and relationships. Same Day Dental opened in Wasilla, Alaska, in July 2013. Dr Cole was finally being true to himself. The first question he greets every patient with is, 'What can we do for you today?'

A typical dental practice using traditional advertising can expect to attract ten to fifteen new patients a month. Many practices spend 5 to 10 percent of their revenue on advertising. Same Day Dental attracts eighty to a hundred new patients a month, by word of mouth and on the strength of their Google reviews. The practice's marketing budget of 1.5 percent of revenues goes towards community event sponsorships, gifts, printing and website maintenance. Fifteen percent of Same Day Dental's production is done free of charge—that's $300,000 worth of services like X-rays, new patient examinations, and diagnostics. All new adult patients and most children are offered a complimentary exam and diagnostics. The financial barrier to a thorough exam is eliminated, so new patients don't experience the additional anxiety about the unknown cost of seeking treatment. The practice has the opportunity to present urgent treatment options, along with elective treatments to be considered in the future. This generous business strategy increases patient acceptance of needed dental care.

VALUES
Guiding beliefs

- 'Transparency
- Fairness
- Empathy
- Gratitude
- Humility'

PURPOSE
Reason to exist

'To improve the health of our community'.

VISION
Aspiration for the future

'Leave the valley in better health than when we came.'

STRATEGY
Aligning opportunities, plans and behaviour

- Offer a same-day dentistry service in a boutique practice, where the majority of treatment is completed in one day.
- Double down on offering a great patient experience and building those relationships.
- Work with the patient's schedule, not the optimum schedule for the practice.
- Make listening to the patient a priority. Structure the consultation around this.
- Spend less than 1.5 percent of revenue on traditional marketing (maintaining our website).

- Contribute to local community charities and projects like Little League.
- Focus on word-of-mouth marketing.
- Deliver on our promise.
- Thank the patients for their trust and the privilege of treating them.
- Reward the whole team for their efforts by introducing a profit sharing model.
- Create a fee structure that's the same for every patient regardless of insurance.

PRESENT AND FUTURE

A typical bread-and-butter solo dental practice can expect to generate revenues in the range of $300,000 to 800,000 a year. Here's what Same Day Dental's revenues looked like during the first four years:

Year 1: $513,000
Year 2: $1.4 million
Year 3: $1.7 million
Year 4: $2.0 million

But what's more important to Dr Cole is that he is finally building the practice he always wanted and making a positive impact on his team, his colleagues and the local community.

FINLAND'S BABY WELCOME KITS

BACKSTORY
Journey to now

A remarkable government initiative that was launched almost eighty years ago has become a tradition in Finland and part of the Finnish identity. It's the Maternity Package—a kit gifted by Kela (the Finnish social security department) to expectant or adoptive parents. The kit was introduced in 1938 to help parents from low-income families and has been given to all expectant mothers regardless of income since 1949. The box itself can be transformed into a crib. Inside the package are around fifty products—necessities like nappies, bedding, and baby clothes, the things parents will need in the baby's first year of life. The contents are updated every year. A mother can choose to receive the Maternity Package or a cash grant, but 95 percent choose the kit.

The catalyst for the launch of the initiative was the country's high infant mortality rates; the government was looking for a way to ensure that women got adequate prenatal care. The prerequisite for receiving the kit was a visit to the doctor before the fourth month of pregnancy.

The program resulted in decreased infant mortality rates, which health professionals attribute to improved prenatal and postnatal care. Finland's maternity care is known to be world class, and the Maternity Package program is now considered a part of the culture of Finland.

VALUES
Guiding beliefs

* Equality
* Community
* Egalitarianism
* Humility
* Respect

PURPOSE
Reason to exist

Improve healthcare for all pregnant women and mothers.

VISION
Aspiration for the future

Give all children a more equal start to life.

STRATEGY
Aligning opportunities, plans and behaviour

* Distribute the Maternity Package to all pregnant women within their first four months of pregnancy.
* Provide free maternity care.
* Schedule early first appointments to monitor and improve care.
* Provide an average of ten to fifteen appointments during a normal pregnancy.
* Encourage women to report problems or concerns early.
* Give midwives and doctors strategies to encourage regular ante-natal visits.

- Raise expectations about maternity care in the community.

PRESENT AND FUTURE

Each year the Finnish government gives away about 40,000 of the boxes, which come with bedding and about fifty other baby items, including clothes, socks, a warm coat and even a baby balaclava for the icy Nordic winter. Finland is the best country in the world for mothers, according to Save the Children's 'State of the World's Mothers' report.

JAMES DAY WEDDING PHOTOGRAPHY

BACKSTORY
Journey to now

What does a self-described 'fat awkward kid' who doesn't know how to connect with people end up doing with his life? James Day was brought up in Arimdale, New South Wales. His childhood was defined by a number of things. First was his father's profession as a lecturer in accounting, which gave the family an opportunity to travel the world. Second was his father's illness. When James was just seven years old, his dad was diagnosed with liver cancer. His family lived in the shadow of the disease for the next seven years, dealing with a transplant and treatment, always living with the knowledge that today might be the day they lost him. Lastly, James inherited his dad's love of photography. He remembers family trips overseas. His dad photographed the landscapes and he photographed the people in them. When they got back from a trip, they processed the photos, and the family would sit around the table with a blank scrapbook and re-create the story they wanted to remember about their latest adventure.

James remembers the last conversation he had with his dad. He was fourteen and wanted to know what he should do with his life. He asked his dad's advice the night before he died.

'Look, Jimbo, don't get yourself a desk,' he said. 'Choose a job that allows you to get out and travel and meet people.' When James asked him what he wished he'd done, he wasn't surprised by the answer. 'I wish I'd been a photographer or a TV cameraman.'

James doesn't remember a time when he didn't have a camera in his hand. He got his first, a Minolta that cost $800 (a fortune at the time), when he was ten, after a year of waiting and talking it over with his dad. He remembers shooting his sister's wedding with that camera soon after their dad died. He still has it today. James did his first paid wedding shoot when he was eighteen—the local bank manager and dental receptionist were getting married and hired James to record their day. He stayed up all night working on and processing the 1621 images he'd taken. The next day, he arrived at their post-wedding family breakfast with the photos. The clients were blown away, and news travelled throughout town about the energetic, passionate photographer kid who would go the extra mile. James's mum took over where his dad left off—matching his earnings dollar for dollar, helping him to buy equipment and build his business, while he also did other jobs like dishwashing and telemarketing to make ends meet.

VALUES
Guiding beliefs

- 'Connection
- Trust
- Empathy
- Fun
- Adventure'

PURPOSE
Reason to exist

'To remind people of the love that exists in their lives'.

VISION
Aspiration for the future

'Enable the gift of human connection'.

STRATEGY
Aligning opportunities, plans and behaviour

- Specialise in bespoke wedding photography.
- Work with adventurous people in adventurous places.
- Develop a journalistic style that captures the real, often unplanned moments of the day that make the occasion memorable.
- Specialise in tangible over digital images.
- Prioritise quality at every stage, from service to production.
- Work only with clients who have an adventurous worldview (the kind of brides who don't mind getting their dresses dirty) and are not just driven by budget.

- Make sure couples feel loved, cared for and respected on the day.
- Allow the photography to add to the experience rather than interfere with it. Give the couple a reason to want to kiss each other (not just instructions to do so for a photo).
- Rely mainly on word-of-mouth marketing.
- Create strong social media profiles.
- Develop partnerships with wedding venues.
- Deliver images quickly.
- Use premium finishes and packaging, with silk ribbon and a meaningful thank-you card.
- Adopt premium pricing, starting at twice the national average for wedding photographers.

PRESENT AND FUTURE

Fourteen years on, James has built a thriving bespoke wedding photography business. He is highly regarded in his industry, teaching photography workshops and delivering speeches. James's special talent for photographing people in landscapes and his unique way of creating and capturing some of the most intimate moments of connection in a couple's life means that he is highly sought after. He accepts only thirty-five wedding bookings a year. There's no doubt about how proud his father would be about the work he does.

THE VIRGIN GROUP

BACKSTORY
Journey to now

The Virgin Group has been challenging the status quo across many industries for decades. My favourite backstory from their suite of brands is the legendary origin story of Virgin Atlantic. In the 1980s, renowned British entrepreneur Richard Branson was stranded in Puerto Rico en route to the British Virgin Islands because of a flight cancellation. Ever resourceful, Richard chartered a small plane, borrowed a blackboard and chalk, and sold the empty seats to stranded fellow passengers. The sign read, 'Virgin Airlines, $39 one way to BVI'.

That incident may have been the genesis of the disruptive airline. Branson was fed up with airlines that didn't care about their passengers. His goal was to challenge the status quo by offering an airline that would provide a good experience and good value for customers. Branson's family had a track record as pioneers in aviation. His uncle was a pilot in World War II, and his mother, Eve, was a stewardess on the first commercial jet in the 1940s. One of Branson's childhood heroes was a Royal Airforce pilot named Douglas Bader. He lost both his legs in a crash early in his career, but went on to fly fighter planes during WWII. After seeing the movie 'Reach for the Sky', which told Bader's heroic story, Richard asked his father about the RAF motto, Per ardua ad astra. 'When he told me that it meant "Through adversity to the stars," I thought the idea of battling one's way to the stars at all costs was the most inspiring thing I'd ever heard.'

Virgin Atlantic started with just one aircraft, a second-hand 747 bought from Boeing. The airline has gone on to pioneer onboard services, like individual TVs and Premium Economy seating, that are now standard on all airlines.

VALUES
Guiding beliefs

- Heartfelt service
- Delight
- Surprise
- Straight up
- Insatiable curiosity
- Smart disruption

PURPOSE
Reason to exist

'Changing business for good'.

VISION
Aspiration for the future

'The end of business as usual'.

'Business has the power to drive change. The time is right for a radically different approach to business—one that puts people and planet at the core of how business is done.'

STRATEGY
Aligning opportunities, plans and behaviour

- Think about the long-term impact of the business decisions that we make today.

- Have a clearly articulated, embedded and measurable purpose in every Virgin business that drives their decisions and fuels their success, resulting in positive impacts on customers, communities and the environment.
- Embed our purpose, principles, and values in all existing and new business investments.
- Pioneer systemic change beyond the Virgin Group through Sir Richard Branson's profile and advocacy as a global business leader and by rising to challenges.
- Create the B Team, a not-for-profit initiative formed by a global group of business leaders to catalyse a better way of doing business, for the wellbeing of people and the planet.

PRESENT AND FUTURE

The Virgin Group's 69,000 staff serve 530 million customers across more than sixty businesses, generating more than 16 billion pounds in revenue annually.

THE MICHELIN GROUP

BACKSTORY
Journey to now

André and Edouard Michelin were seventeen and eleven when their father died. They and their sister, Marie, were raised with a strong set of values by their mother, Adèle. André once told his grandchildren that his mother said, 'Personal profit is meaningless. Your duty is to cultivate the gifts you have received and put them to good use for the benefit of all, without asking what you will get in return.'

The two brothers ran a rubber factory in Clermont-Ferrand in the late 1880s. One day, a cyclist whose pneumatic bicycle tyre needed repair showed up at their door asking for help. In those days, tyres were glued to the wheel rim and could take hours to remove and repair. When Édouard tested the repaired tyre the following day, it failed within a few hundred metres. This incident inspired the brothers to create a tyre that would not need to be glued to the wheel rim. Michelin took out its first patent for a removable pneumatic tyre in 1891. The cyclist, Charles Terront, went on to win the world's first long-distance cycle race, the 1891 Paris–Brest–Paris race, using the new technology.

In addition to manufacturing tyres, Michelin created and distributed guides for drivers to help them to find hotels, mechanics and fuel throughout France. You could say that the company was one of the world's first content marketers. At that time, the country didn't even have an extensive road system and it's estimated that only 2,200 people owned a car.

VALUES
Guiding beliefs

'Respect, first and foremost, for people and the environment, our customers, our partners and our shareholders. Respect for our employees with decent work conditions, equality and diversity. Respect for our suppliers with whom we want to maintain long-term, transparent and demanding relationships.'

'Progress too, which we believe should never stop'.

'And finally, the love of a job well done. The desire to fully explore our ideas and our convictions, to make them a reality'.

PURPOSE
Reason to exist

'To find a better way forward for everyone'.

'Because we believe that mobility is essential for human development, we are innovating passionately to make it safer, more efficient and more environmentally friendly.'

VISION
Aspiration for the future

Be the leader in sustainable mobility.

'Imagine a future in which your tire is also a wheel: puncture-proof because there is no pressure. Its ruggedness comes from its biomimetic structure, as if it had been created by Nature... A wheel made of recycled materials and which is completely recycled at the end of its life, after having covered thousands and thousands of kilometers—as long as the vehicle itself. Now imagine that you don't have to worry any more about keeping your loved ones safe when you travel, because road conditions and bad weather don't matter any more: your tread instantly adjusts to your driving conditions, whenever necessary, using just the right amount of materials. A tread that can be modified and replenished at will, without wasting any resources, time or money, and which protects the environment for the generations to come...'

STRATEGY
Aligning opportunities, plans and behaviour

- 'Strengthen customer satisfaction.
- Encourage employee achievement.
- Provide solid financial performance.
- Innovate to reinforce the leadership of our products and services.
- Become a benchmark as a responsible company.
- Contribute to the development of local communities and sustainable mobility.'

PRESENT AND FUTURE

Michelin's headquarters are still in Clermont-Ferrand, France. The business has a presence in 170 countries and employs more than 111,000 people. The company produced 187 million tyres in 2016 and is working towards its vision of helping to create an economy capable of protecting the planet's resources.

> *Michelin's vision of future mobility is also based on a vision of the entire economy that guides our Research and our innovations. A circular economy capable of protecting the planet's resources by reducing, reusing, renewing or recycling the materials required to manufacture our products, and avoid leaving a negative impact on the environment. This approach has been dubbed the '4R Strategy' at Michelin, for Reduce, Reuse, Recycle and Renew. We bear in mind that, for mobility to have a bright future, it will have to be ever safer, more efficient and more environmentally friendly.*

IKEA

BACKSTORY
Journey to now

Visionary entrepreneur Ingvar Kamprad founded IKEA in 1943 when he was just seventeen. He was raised on a farm in the Småland region of Sweden, and that's where his global business empire began. Journalist Oliver Burkeman describes the region as 'a windswept, hardscrabble place, breeding in its inhabitants an austerity and make-do attitude that IKEA has simply made global'.

Kamprad started selling matches to his neighbours at the age of five. By the time he was seven, he'd discovered he could buy matches in bulk cheaply in Stockholm, re-sell them at a low price, and still make a decent profit. He began using his bicycle to reach customers who were further afield. Kamprad eventually expanded his product range to include seeds, pencils, greeting cards and Christmas decorations.

Kamprad, who was dyslexic, used a small sum of money given to him by his father for doing well at school to start his mail order business. He named his company IKEA—an acronym using the initials of his own name and the first letters of the farm Elmataryd, where he was brought up, and Agunnaryd, his hometown. (And it was through names that Kamprad would further demonstrate his skill of turning lemons into lemonade. When his dyslexia made remembering product codes confusing, he created the unique IKEA product naming system. Products are named in Swedish according to type. Rugs are named after towns in Sweden and Denmark. Beds are given names of towns in Norway. And shelves are named after boys or occupations.)

He used local milk trucks as delivery vehicles to save money. Kamprad's first furniture product was a replica of his uncle Ernst's kitchen table, which had been manufactured locally. When the local manufacturers started boycotting Kamprad's business to protest his low prices, he began designing in-house. The revolutionary flat-pack furniture concept came years later when a frustrated young draftsman who worked for IKEA, Chris Lundgren, decided to pull the legs off a kitchen table so he could get it into the boot of his car. By cutting down on assembly and shipping costs, the flat-pack concept enabled Kamprad to fulfil his mission of bringing affordable, stylish, quality furniture to more people. The first IKEA store opened in Älmhult in 1958; the company is still headquartered there today. IKEA's former president, Anders Dahlvig, explained the decision not to move away: 'You have to stay grounded. You need your history.'

In 1976, Kamprad wrote 'Testament of a Furniture Dealer'—an extraordinary eight-page manifesto outlining his vision and business philosophy (the PDF is still available online today). This is part of what Kamprad says in the opening paragraphs of the document:

> *Part of creating a better everyday life for the many people also consists of breaking free from status and convention—becoming freer as human beings. We aim to make our name synonymous with that concept too— for our own benefit and for the inspiration of others. We must, however, always bear in mind that freedom implies responsibility, meaning that we must demand much of ourselves.*

According to former CEO Peter Agnefjäll, a key factor in the company's strong performance is that they have a long-term view and don't aim to maximise short-term profits.

VALUES
Guiding beliefs

- 'Togetherness
- Caring for people and planet
- Cost-consciousness
- Simplicity
- Renew and improve
- Different with a meaning
- Give and take responsibility
- Lead by example'

PURPOSE
Reason to exist

'To create a better everyday life for the many people'.

VISION
Aspiration for the future

Benefit the many.

STRATEGY
Aligning opportunities, plans and behaviour

- Offer a wide range of well-designed, functional home furnishing products at prices so low that as many people as possible will be able to afford them.

- Optimise our entire value chain, by building long-term supplier relationships, investing in highly automated production and producing large volumes.
- Grow by using our own resources. We earn our money before we spend it.
- Make long-term investments for the future.
- Ensure that IKEA is accessible, so that more people can create a better everyday life at home.
- Create a franchise business model that allows the company to expand while allowing us to remain independent.
- Re-invest a majority of our profits in existing and new IKEA stores, as well as in product development, sustainable solutions and by continuously lowering prices.
- Switch our entire lighting range to energy-efficient LED.
- Source all the cotton we use in our products from more sustainable sources.
- Work towards 100 percent renewable energy by producing as much as we consume in our operations—sourcing all of our wood from more sustainable sources by 2020.
- Commit to adding up to EUR 1 billion for climate action.

PRESENT AND FUTURE

An article published in The Guardian in 2004 reported that an estimated 10 percent of Europe's population was conceived in an IKEA bed. In 2016, 783 million people visited an IKEA store and IKEA.com was visited more than 2 billion times. By 2017, IKEA had 400 stores in 49 countries. IKEA estimates that by 2020 it will serve 1.5 billion visitors a year in 500 stores.

HEAT HOLDERS THERMAL SOCKS

BACKSTORY
Journey to now

The city of Leicester has been the home of the British sock and hosiery industry for two hundred years. It was there that Charles Henry Doughty began work as a sock presser at Clarendon Dye Works before WWII. His wife, Amelia, worked in the same factory as a sock turner. Some socks had to be dyed inside out, so they needed people (it was mostly women who did this job back then) to turn the socks inside out and then turn them back again once they'd been dyed.

Their son, Victor Charles Doughty, went to work for Bentley Engineering, who built the Bentley Komet sock machines in 1954—the same year his son, David Charles Doughty, was born. Victor eventually became foreman on the shop floor at Bentley's. He was there for approximately forty years, before being made redundant in the 1990s during the decline of textile manufacturing in England.

David left school at fifteen, in 1969, and went to work as an apprentice at D. Byford & Co Ltd. He was training to be a mechanic and learned knitting technology, studying two days a week at Leicester Polytechnic. David left Byfords in 1978 and went to work for Pex Socks in Leicester, but was made redundant in 1980. In 1981, he started his own sock-making business (MarkShane Ltd) with a single sock machine in his father's garage. Victor was an engineer who could help with the installation and operation of the sock machines. Within a decade David had 300 people working for him.

There was an expectation that David's sons, who spent their school holidays working at the factory, would join him in running the business one day. But as prices and profit margins were driven down by cheaper overseas labour, it was impossible for the factory to remain viable as it was. David sold the factory and went into partnership with the Ruias, a family of second-generation Indian immigrants. Together they pivoted and became the sock importers Drew Brady. David's son Shane joined the company in 1995, becoming the first member of the fourth generation to join the sock business.

The team built a successful company for many years, importing generic socks, until the retailers they sold to decided to maximise profits by cutting out the middle man and go direct to overseas manufacturers. Since their product wasn't unique, they constantly found themselves competing on price. They all knew this was not a sustainable business strategy. Having to compete on price meant compromising on quality—the only way to do that was to make poorer socks. This didn't sit well with a family that had been making socks for generations.

David had his epiphany while watching his son play rugby on a bitter February day. Surrounded by spectators who were stamping their feet in an attempt to stay warm, he began to wonder why their company couldn't just make great socks that kept people warm. He was sure people would pay for a superior product. He also felt that his company had lost sight of their purpose in their attempt to compete and survive. They were no longer doing work they were proud to have done. Armed with this insight, David and the team at Drew Brady went back to the drawing board and began to ask a different question. What if instead of trying to make a cheaper thermal sock, they tried to make the warmest thermal sock in the world?

This question led the team on a passionate two-year R&D journey, in collaboration with their manufacturers in Jakarta, to reinvent the thermal sock. As a result, they developed Heat Holders, the warmest thermal socks in the world.

VALUES
Guiding beliefs

- Quality and innovation
- Passion and pride
- Care and wellbeing of our customers and employees
- Entrepreneurial
- The little thing that makes a big difference

PURPOSE
Reason to exist

'To create the little things that have a big impact on people's days'.

VISION
Aspiration for the future

'Create a portfolio of better products that solve everyday problems.'

STRATEGY
Aligning opportunities, plans and behaviour

* Innovate by solving a genuine customer problem.
* Never compete on price = Never compromise for price.
* Quality first.
* Act with empathy.
* Do work we're proud to have done.
* Only create the extraordinary.

PRESENT AND FUTURE

When Heat Holders launched in 2008, the sceptics said nobody would pay 'five quid' for one pair of thermal socks. They were wrong! Twenty million pairs of Heat Holders have been sold in more than thirty countries since then. The company not only serves people in colder climates, but has also gone on to develop more specialist socks that solve problems for people with medical issues and extra durability requirements. Today the company innovates from a place of empathy.

SMALL GIANTS

BACKSTORY
Journey to now

I remember when I first heard Berry Liberman tell her story at an event in Queensland. It began as a heroic tale of triumph in the face of adversity, the story of how her paternal grandfather—a Holocaust survivor and 'refugee entrepreneur'—migrated to Melbourne and built a thriving business. He worked during the day, and at night would walk the back laneways of the city, salvaging damaged silk stockings (with permission) from the rubbish that had been discarded by the factories. He and his wife repaired them at their kitchen table; then he sold them at a discount. By the time the factories realised what was happening, Berry's grandfather had saved enough money to buy his own factory. This was the start of what would grow into a hugely successful family empire built on the back of an incredible work ethic. Berry's father and his brother also worked in the business. Their business was all consuming. Work and family were inseparable. The Libermans went on to become one of Australia's wealthiest families.

The turning point in Berry's life was her father's sudden death at the age of forty-five. She was fifteen, and his death had a deep impact on her. Berry had seen him driven to work incredibly hard to achieve in an attempt to live up to the start his father had made for the family. He was always working. When she read his letters ten years later, she discovered that he was just starting to question whether the life that had been created for him was the one he really wanted. Berry and her siblings inherited the family fortune, but her question was always how she would create meaning for herself. 'Compared to the massiveness of what I had inherited, everything I did seemed little.' Berry also observed the children of other incredibly successful entrepreneurs and noticed that the 'curse of inheritance stripped them of their identity, purpose and mission in life'.

Berry was on a mission of her own. She wanted to be a successful Hollywood screenwriter, walk the red carpet at the Oscars and bring home a golden statue one day. After she finished university, she went to Hollywood to pursue that dream. Five years in, she realised she was working for external validation. What would happen even if she did win the Oscar? Then what? Meeting her future husband, Danny Almagor, a 'deep humanitarian' who was interested in bigger questions (and who founded Engineers Without Borders in Australia), prompted Berry to ask her own questions about what she wanted from life and what she hoped to leave behind.

VALUES
Guiding beliefs
- People come first.
- Everyone can find passion and meaning in their work and life.
- No one is an island.
- There is enough for every person's need, but not for every person's greed.
- Business can be a force for good.

PURPOSE
Reason to exist

To create, support and empower social enterprises.

VISION
Aspiration for the future

To use business to change the world.

STRATEGY
Aligning opportunities, plans and behaviour

- Invest in a portfolio of businesses that create holistic value for all stakeholders.
- Invest across the spectrum of returns in order to create the deepest regenerative and sustainable impact.
- Focus on impact creation while maintaining commercial sustainability.
- Measure our portfolio's contribution by using rigorous independent certifications and metrics in order to hold ourselves and our partners accountable.
- Continuously learn, evolve and improve our impacts, on ourselves, each other and the planet.
- Shift our communities towards empathy and the new economy.

PRESENT AND FUTURE

Berry and Danny have gone on to build a life and have a family. Their joint passions for the environment, human rights, justice, art, creativity, business and creating meaningful experiences led them to start Small Giants, an investment fund that supports and nurtures business and other organisations that have the potential to change the world—to be great, not just big. Small Giants was founded on the premise that business can be a powerful tool of change in the world.

MELBOURNE'S HAPPIEST TRAM DRIVER

BACKSTORY
Journey to now

It's hard to imagine starting work for a bank as a teenage boy, at a time when one of the rules in the employee handbook was that men should always wear a hat to the office. That's what Bruce Whalley remembers from his first job, which was at the State Bank of Victoria in Melbourne. Back then just three details were handwritten on the outside of your personnel file: your name, employee number and religion. It was a time when women were paid a little more than half a man's salary for doing the same job and you had to count the $12 million in cash on hand at the branch three times a year.

Bruce, the eldest of four children, was an adored grandson of farming folk and servicemen who were WWI veterans. His people were self-made, fifth-generation Australians who were good with their hands and generous with their hearts. They had time for people. Bruce grew up in the suburbs of Melbourne and at first thought he would have a career on the land or in forestry. But in 1970, at the age of sixteen, he was offered a job in the bank. The pay was $33 a week, three times what an apprentice would make. A career in the bank was a career for life. Your future was secure and mapped out;

eventually you would become a bank manager and retire with a good pension. Bruce was keen to learn and loved the culture of service and connection with customers. It was not unusual for someone from the bank to go grocery shopping for a sick pensioner, then deliver her groceries and get her signature on a withdrawal slip for the funds. It was a time when customers were customers for life and bank tellers had pistols that they took apart and cleaned at morning tea. Bruce worked at the bank for eighteen years.

In his twenties, he saved hard for an overseas trip, working four other jobs to get enough money for an eighteen-month adventure to Europe with his mate Larry. He reckons that $6,000 would have bought him a house in Melbourne at the time. The friends travelled all over Europe and ended up living in a Hezbollah village in Lebanon. It was quite an education for a twenty-three-year-old with a blinkered, Anglo-Saxon view of the world.

On his return to Australia, Bruce did further training in accounting and lectured part-time in banking and finance to MBA students. He got several promotions, married and had a daughter and a son. Bruce remembers this as a creative and innovative time in banking, when the bank was defining its role as part of the community. He wasn't just marking time; he had to use his brain and make his mark under the guidance of mentors he's grateful for who helped him along the way. Bruce moved up the ladder, transferring to other banks and being promoted to senior roles. The common thread was always that he was there to help people succeed by bringing more of themselves to work. He created a culture where people felt empowered. Eventually Bruce went into independent consulting, training and marketing. He was a founding member of what is now the Customer Contact Management Association.

In his late fifties, Bruce had a motorcycle accident, ending up with a badly busted knee; during his hospitalisation, the medical team discovered that he also had prostate cancer. He spent a year in treatment and recovering with little else to do but think about what he wanted from the next chapter of his life. A close friend was a tram driver, and they got chatting over coffee one day about the old days, when tram drivers and conductors sang and did magic tricks to entertain passengers along their routes. Bruce began to wonder if he could re-create his nostalgic vision of tramming, of people like the tram driver Lenny Bates who did more than just sell tickets. They made tramming an experience.

Bruce decided he wanted to give it a try, applied, passed the medical exam and got the job. As a former lecturer, he was used to having an audience. Bruce says he doesn't mind if the audience is in front of him or behind him. Those lucky enough to travel on his tram are constantly surprised and delighted. Bruce believes that people don't want much. He's constantly amazed that the bar to delight is so low that his dad jokes can brighten people's days. Of course, he's selling himself short. Bruce puts a ton of effort into bringing himself to work every day. He creates a unique culture on his tram and sees his role as more than just getting people from A to B. It's an opportunity to have a positive impact on their day and create community.

VALUES
Guiding beliefs

- Personal pride
- Fun
- Connection
- Encouragement
- Community
- Empathy

PURPOSE
Reason to exist

To encourage.

VISION
Aspiration for the future

Change people's perspectives.

STRATEGY
Aligning opportunities, plans and behaviour

- Learn phrases in different languages, including Japanese, Arabic, Italian, Spanish, German, Dutch, Russian, Greek, Chinese, Mandarin, Korean, Cantonese, and Hindi (Bruce recites a New Year greeting in thirty languages).
- Deliberate practice. Consider the ideal outcome you want to achieve.
- Help people to get the most out of the experience and the city.

- Keep up to date with what's going on in the city or in the news and sports.
- Encourage community and bonding (for example, by singing 'happy birthday').
- Help passengers at tram stops with directions.
- Find commonalities between people of all ages and all cultures.
- Help foster a sense of pride in our city.
- Lead by example.
- Break down barriers.
- Change the culture.

PRESENT AND FUTURE

If you're lucky enough to ride Bruce's tram one day, don't be surprised if he gets everyone singing happy birthday to a commuter, or gives you the best guided tour of the city, or you hear him greeting an elderly Chinese couple in Mandarin. The first time I rode on his tram, he reminded everyone on board that we were lucky enough to live in the World's Most Liveable City. 'Six times running, ladies and gentlemen. This is no flash in the pan,' he said. That was over two years ago and I still remember the grins spreading through the tram.

FIASCO GELATO

BACKSTORY
Journey to now

James Boettcher is the kind of guy who people are immediately drawn to. His warmth and passion are infectious. Growing up poor in Calgary, Alberta, in a single-parent household, he always had part-time jobs to help put a few dollars on the table so he and his father could afford to eat. He shovelled snow from sidewalks when he was eight and started bagging groceries at a natural foods store on his fourteenth birthday—both decisions that James believes with hindsight were about determining his own fate and making a difference.

Eventually it all became too great to bear. By the time he was fifteen, James began to understand the reasons his childhood was financially challenging and why the eviction notices came every other month. His father was trying to get them one step ahead by heading to the casino; instead he put them further behind. He found it difficult to manage money, and James's constant contribution almost enabled the situation to continue. James tried everything to help his father to get better with money, including enrolling other family members, but to no avail. The habit was too strong to break without hitting rock bottom. It was then that James realised that if he was going to change the outcome for both himself and his father, he'd have to leave home and the father he adored. His decision was supported by his grandfather and aunt, but that didn't make it any easier:

*'My dad and I are and always will be a team. We
have gone through everything together. But at that
moment of entering high school and knowing the
environment I was living in would impact this, I
made a choice to pack up the few things that were
most important to me and take up my aunt's offer
to rent a room in her basement and contribute
financially to her household.'*

In high school, James got into design by accident. The
school was unique in that it was self-directed; students
had a lot of autonomy and could often choose what they
wanted to learn. During an art class one day, students were
instructed to draw a cat. James wanted to draw something
different, but his teacher refused to allow him, so he decided
to leave the class. As he was leaving, he saw a kid drawing on
a computer, using Adobe Illustrator software. James pulled
up a chair. Next thing he knew, he was designing material
for the drama club and becoming fascinated with logos. He
began to pay attention to package design, logos and fonts
on the products in the store as he was bagging groceries.
He started to explore to discover the intention behind the
designs and to learn how branding worked. Before long, he
started a design company from his bedroom.

James continued to work in retail grocery stores through
high school (he became assistant manager of a store when he
was just seventeen). He first got involved with Fiasco Gelato
in 2003, when a friend's brother decided to open a 'small
gelato scoop shop' in Calgary, where it's winter for half of the
year. James worked with him on design and brand strategy.
Six years later, James was offered the opportunity to buy the

business because James's passion for Fiasco was greater than anyone else's involved. Aged twenty-five, with just $1800 in his bank account, James shook hands on the deal to acquire 'the little gelato business that could'. James streamlined Fiasco from four stores to a single storefront and reinvented the brand. Two days before he was due to open Fiasco 2.0, a fire gutted the store, and with only six months left on the lease he had to rethink his business strategy. He found a garage and later a hundred-foot commissary space where he could start production again in 2010. James got orders on Fridays, spent the weekends making gelato, and then pushed a chest freezer into a rental van on Mondays to make his deliveries.

Fiasco makes its own gelato, which seems like a ridiculous thing to highlight as a point of difference, but in the grocery industry, many brands either hire a co-packer to make the product or license their name to someone who wants to make it.

In 2012 James and the team at Fiasco stopped simply thinking of themselves as 'the little gelato shop that could' and began working towards a vision to be 'a wholesale purveyor of some of the finest Italian Ice Cream in Canada—with a commitment to changing the way business is done'. They consciously 'put people and purpose above all else and thought more about [their] community.' For example:

> *It's very easy and affordable for us to throw everything in the garbage, instead of sorting it. ... But before we existed, that amount of garbage didn't exist. And so, it's our responsibility now to figure out how to divert, compost and recycle as much as possible.*

127

They have hit some bumps on their journey to their new 'Willy Wonka meets Google' factory and headquarters. There was another fire at their new premises and financial woes during an economic downturn. James opted to reduce his salary to a $1 for three months and asked the six top performers on his team to take a 10 percent salary reduction, as well as miss a pay period, so that no one who deserved to be there lost their job. There have been incredible triumphs, too, like the day Wholefoods CEO John Mackie gave James his business card at a book signing and told him to email him when Fiasco was stocked at Wholefoods, which, after countless meetings with and rejections from buyers and distributors, James did three years later. Or the day in 2014 when Fiasco was stocked on the shelves of Sunterra, the store where James began bagging groceries seventeen years earlier. In the nine years since James took over, there has been plenty to celebrate, from business awards to Best Gelato accolades, B Corp certification to fundraising partnerships with charities and local communities in need and the opening of Fiasco's gelato academy. But the biggest win for James and his team is doing something that people care about.

Yes, we started by making delicious, tiny spoonfuls of heaven, and we still do. But our real mission and vision is to have a massive impact on how the world looks at employment, business, and what we deserve as consumers. We just happen to do it by making gelato.

VALUES
Guiding beliefs

- 'We are obsessed with quality and integrity.
- We are connected to our customers' community and environment.
- We will always be innovative and creative.
- We lead with love, respect and selflessness.
- We actively embrace, growth, wellness and betterment.
- We are proactive in maintaining our financial stability.
- We have the courage to own our mistakes and learn from them.
- We won't forget where we came from.'
- Fiasco holds a 'Core Values' awards ceremony every year to ensure that these values are not simply posters on the wall—they guide every single decision the company makes.

PURPOSE
Reason to exist

'In our constant & unwavering pursuit for greatness, we are committed to enriching people's lives one tiny spoonful at a time.' This purpose statement takes up a whole wall in Fiasco's 'Willy Wonka meets Google' factory.

Enriching people's lives is all-encompassing; it involves every decision and step of the process in what we do, where we get to choose whether or not what we do is enriching someone's life. And when you realize that power and choice, you get to decide. So, when you decide to offer unlimited paid time off to your team so they never have to worry about exploration or what life might throw their way, or when you decide to pay 100% of your people a living wage, you know that every part of their journey is enriched.

VISION
Aspiration for the future

To continue to change the way the grocery world operates and [show] how employers and entrepreneurs can look at doing business differently.

STRATEGY
Aligning opportunities, plans and behaviour

- Create the best product possible, honouring the historical craft and care of gelato. Because people don't deserve sales and marketing, they deserve better.
- Use real ingredients, sourced as locally as possible (with the exception of nuts from the homeland of gelato, and fruits that are regionally specific).
- Reduce sugars and find natural alternatives that don't detract from the construct of the product.
- Operate at the high end of the market, where customers are prepared to pay a premium.
- Run a business that looks after its people, the environment, and its customers; we must not race to the bottom.
- Invest resources in unique branding and packaging.
- Use 100% post-consumer plastic.
- Aim to build a loyal customer base that we call fans, not customers.

- Demonstrate our unwavering commitment to social and environmental impact by becoming a B Corp and adhering to the standards that demonstrate who we are as a company.
- Treat everyone at every level of our daily operations with dignity, love, and respect, by doing the right thing, like paying people a living wage.
- Acknowledge that we have not come this far just to come this far.
- Use that purpose to fuel continual growth with the intention of changing the world.
- Use that money to be even better at producing a product that matters for everyone.
- While doing above, be steadfast in our culture of this being bigger than us and have the time of our lives on this journey.

PRESENT AND FUTURE

Today, Fiasco gelato is available in 1600 stores across Canada, outselling Ben & Jerry's in Western Canada. The brand is quickly becoming a household name because of the company's approach to doing business differently. James's team has grown to fifty-two strong—one of whom is his dad. Fiasco has recently been acknowledged as an emerging cult brand alongside brands like Reddit and Soul Cycle.

'We have grown almost 6000% since founding Fiasco 2.0 nine years ago, and attribute this success to one guiding principle—do what is right and the money will come.'

PART THREE
Developing Your Story-Driven Strategy

*'The one thing that you have that nobody else
has is you. Your voice, your mind, your story,
your vision.'*
—*Neil Gaiman*

In this section of the book, you will find prompts that walk you through the different stages of the Story-Driven Framework. They are designed to nudge you in the right direction. You should also add your burning questions, prompts, insights and stories about things that are important to you and your team. You can work through the prompts alone, with a partner or in groups within your team. You'll need quiet uninterrupted time and pen and paper or your favourite note-taking app.

It's tempting to skip this step or to think you're not making an impact because you're not setting out to change the world for millions of people. Often, though, it's the person with the lowest rank in an organisation who has the chance to make the biggest impact day-to-day. A receptionist who understands the unique contribution she has to make in the lives of a customer or patient can change everything.

One of the most inspiring people I know is a guy called Mark Dyck, who ran a tiny community bakery in Regina, Saskatchewan. Mark created a weekly giveaway of a free bread basket that the recipient had to pass on to a friend. His work didn't just feed people's bellies—it fed their souls. So, don't be afraid to dig deep on these questions regardless of your job title, reservations or fears. Change doesn't only happen with the stroke of the pen of people in positions of power. It happens one person at a time when we have the courage to look each other in the eye and act with empathy and intention.

BACKSTORY
Your story

An epiphany of some kind has been the catalyst for many an entrepreneurial journey. Emma Bridgewater's sudden realisation that there was a gap in the everyday crockery market when she was looking for the perfect birthday present for her mother. The first time Jack Ma typed the word 'beer' into a Google search and found no Chinese results. This is the place where I'd invite you to begin retracing your steps on your journey to now—to reflect on the events, incidents and stories that changed your mind, your feelings or your direction in life and work. Those happenings have been the making of you.

1. *What's the hardest thing you've ever done?*
   Record the story of the time—the
   circumstances and events leading up to your
   decision and what you experienced at the time.

2. *What did doing the hard thing teach you
   about yourself?*
   How have you used that learning to make hard
   decisions or to solve problems?

3. *Who are the two people who have had the biggest
   impact on your life?*
   Can you remember and record a story about
   how they changed the way you saw the world?
   (I want to give a shout-out here to librarians
   because I've heard countless stories from
   entrepreneurs and writers about a librarian who
   changed their lives.)

4. *What did you learn from them?*
   What events in your life show how you
   have applied the lessons you learned from
   those mentors?

5. *What was your first job and what valuable lessons
   did you learn there?*
   Describe the incidents that reveal some of the
   challenges and insights you gained from doing
   this work.

6. *What's your proudest memory? Why?*
   Record that story in as much detail as you
   can remember.

7. *When are you at your best?*
   What's the story that best illustrates that?
   Tell it.

8. *If you could change one thing about yourself, what would that be? Why?*
   Describe an incident where things might have been different if you had been able to change that one thing.

9. *What's the one thing you wouldn't change about yourself? Why?*
   Remember and record a story about how that quality you value enabled you to step up and do something you're proud to have done.

10. *How can you bring more of that thing you wouldn't change into your work?*
    In what everyday situations would it be helpful to bring this quality into play?

11. *Go back in time five years. What's the thing your old self would be most proud that you've achieved?*
    Record a story to explain the reason this event is something to be proud of.

12. *How would you like to be remembered?*
    What event from your life so far best illustrates that you are the person you want to be remembered as? Record that story.

Your company story

1. *Where did the idea for your business or company come from?*
   Describe the time and place and the events surrounding the epiphany. Who was involved? What were they thinking and feeling?

2. *Who were the key players?*
   Record how they met, what they had in common and what they liked about each other.

3. *What influenced you/them?*
   What were the circumstances, incidents, people that shaped the idea?

4. *Why did you/they feel compelled to start this business?*
   What story from your/their past illustrates why you were the person/people to take on this challenge?

5. *What were you/they trying to fix?*
   Tell the story of what you/they hoped you could change for one particular person when you started out on this journey. Be as specific and detailed as you can.

6. *Why did you/they care about this particular problem?*
   Record the before-and-after story of a person who you/they wanted to solve this problem for.

7. *What challenges did you/they have to overcome?*
   Share your most vivid memories of the biggest hurdles.

8. *What were your/their greatest strengths?*
   Share a story about a time where they helped you/them to endure and pull through.

9. *What gives you/them the most pride about the company's impact?*
   Record the story of a customer, event or achievement that best illustrates this.

10. *How would you like your work to be remembered?*
    Record the story someone will share about of your company's impact twenty years from now.

11. *What question should I have asked you?*
    Go ahead and record the answer which reveals the most about your character or business philosophy.

VALUES
Your beliefs

VALUES LIST

Accountability	Achievement	Adaptability
Authenticity	Balance	Bravery
Challenge	Community	Connection
Contribution	Courage	Creativity
Curiosity	Determination	Discipline
Discovery	Empathy	Excellence
Fairness	Family	Freedom
Fun	Flexibility	Generosity
Grace	Gratitude	Growth
Happiness	Harmony	Health
Honesty	Humility	Imagination
Improvement	Individuality	Inventiveness
Joy	Kindness	Leadership

Learning	Love	Loyalty
Mastery	Meaning	Morality
Optimism	Originality	Passion
Persistence	Playfulness	Power
Reliability	Respect	Security
Service	Significance	Success
Teamwork	Tolerance	Transparency
Trust	Understanding	Unity
Vision	Wisdom	Wonder

1. Circle the values that immediately resonate with you or add your own.
2. Why did you choose these particular values?
3. Explain why each of these values is important to you.
4. How do these values influence your decisions, work or business practices? Write a paragraph each about three business strategy decisions that were guided by your values.
5. How have these values served you in the past?
6. Apart from personal integrity, why is it important to live by these values?
7. Write a list of your core values. It's often helpful to start with the word 'I' or 'we' followed by a verb—we act, believe, succeed, care, behave, deliver and so on.

PURPOSE
Your reason

1. What's the thing you're most proud to have done to date?
2. Who inspires you and why?
3. Who influences your work and why?
4. Who would you like to be an inspiration to?
5. What's your audience's or customer's story?
6. If you could achieve only one thing in the next year, what would that be?
7. Why is this goal important to you?
8. What change are you trying to create?
9. What makes your work important to your audience?
10. What's the reason your business exists?

VISION
Your contribution

1. *What change happens in the future because of your work?*
   a) Whom are you affecting?
   b) How are their lives changed for the better?
   Share one or two stories about the kind of people (as they are today) whose lives you hope to change.

2. *What three things do you want to achieve in the next five years and why?*
   Share the reasons why these are important to prioritise.

3. *What will your legacy be?*
   Describe in as much detail as you can how
   the world was changed because your product,
   service or company existed.

STRATEGY
Your plan

WHAT

1. Explain your project or business idea to a stranger.
2. What problems does it solve or need does it meet?
3. What are your goals for this project?
4. Make a list of your strengths and weaknesses.
5. What are your top three near-term goals?
6. What are your specific measures of success?

WHO

1. Describe your target audience or customer.
2. Why does he want or need your product or service?
3. How will he find you?
4. How will you gain his trust, then loyalty?
5. What reasons are you giving him to choose you?
6. How does your work, product or service change his day, life or worldview?

HOW

1. List the first five key practical steps to executing your plan.
2. What resources do you need?

3. What resources do you have?
4. Detail your timeline.
5. What challenges do you envisage?
6. How will you mitigate against these challenges?

ALIGNMENT

1. Explain how your day-to-day strategic decisions represent who and what you or your company stands for. For example, what kinds of opportunities would you pursue or turn down? Record stories and examples.
2. How do you ensure that your words—emails, website copy, presentations and on and on—reflect your values and intention?
3. Are your creative direction, products and services representative of your purpose? Explain how they are supporting your goals.
4. Do your decisions, client list, strategic partnerships and goals align with your vision for the future?

Don't stop there. These questions and prompts are simply your starting point—a way to invite you to make time to reflect more deeply on the change you want to create and the unique contribution you have to make. What's the next most important question you need to ask yourself? Keep going!

CONCLUSION
The Making of Us

'You can't connect the dots looking forward;
you can only connect them looking backward.'
—Steve Jobs

We're so busy trying to connect the dots looking forward, we overlook the opportunity to learn from the experiences, not just the mistakes, of the past. We don't spend as much time looking back as we should. I don't mean just to reminisce about fond memories or to regret stupid mistakes. But rather, to reflect on the significance of our stories, remind ourselves of our resourcefulness and reinforce our sense of identity. History, heritage and hindsight are powerful teachers. But we're in too much of a hurry to reach higher ground to learn from them.

The first poem I could recite was Robert Louis Stevenson's 'My Shadow'. 'I have a little shadow that goes in and out with me...' It occupied, then preoccupied me for days, weeks and months. At first, I didn't believe the poet. I tried to disprove his theory by escaping from the places where my shadow fell. Of course, Stevenson was right; we can't escape our shadows—the same goes for our backstories. And nor should we want to. We can learn a lot about ourselves, the world and our place in it by connecting the dots looking backwards. Instead, we worry about perfecting today's dot or agonise about positioning tomorrow's. We forget to look back at where we've been, to see how far we've come and to understand what that journey has to teach us. We spend our time looking at the dots when we should be searching for the connections between them.

One of our favourite books to read to our boys when they were small was Eric Carle's *The Very Hungry Caterpillar*. First published in 1969, it's sold more than 44 million copies to date. The book tells the story of a caterpillar who hatches from an egg on Sunday, then starts out on a journey. On Monday, he eats an apple but he's still hungry. On Tuesday, he eats two pears, and so on, as he weaves his way through the holes in the pages. The caterpillar spends the week gorging on everything in his path—anything he can get his jaws around—from watermelon to chocolate cake. Then he retreats into his cocoon to sleep. When he wakes, he is a beautiful butterfly.

Like the Hungry Caterpillar, we are all on a journey to metamorphosis. Going through openings. Taking things in, filling ourselves up. Becoming who we were meant to be. One day at a time. And just as the work of the caterpillar was to grow, that's our work too—to have a stronger sense of identity as we progress on our journey.

As children, we are told how unique we are. It's explained that we are a miracle of genetics and chance, just by virtue of our being here. Our parents look into our eyes and we know this to be the truest thing they will ever tell us: 'you are one-of-a-kind'. Then, full of hope and fear, they send us into a world that requires us to fit in and compete, to meet the requirements of a system where conformity is rewarded with gold stars and merit badges.

We were taught how to recognise colours and count to ten. Shown how to hold a spoon and tie our laces. Nagged about table manners and doing homework. Trained to recognise threats in our midst and opportunities when they present themselves. But there was very little instruction about how to become wise to ourselves. We were encouraged to find out what we were good at, but not to figure out what we stood for and how we came to stand for it. We learned the value of making good choices, but not to understand why we felt they were the right ones. We became good at telling people what they wanted to hear and stifled what we wanted to say.

Nobody escapes trying to fit in as they grow up, and all that conforming leaves very little room for the effort that's required to be who we are. I have no idea how many woman-hours are spent applying makeup, straightening hair and looking at the shape of our own biceps and butts in the mirror. But anecdotally I can tell you, from witnessing morning rituals in all their guises at the gym every day, it's more than we care to admit. We spend a lot of time looking at our reflection—not so much to see or acknowledge ourselves, but to wonder how our appearance will be perceived and what we need to do to alter or perfect it. Our days are consumed with measuring up in all kinds of arbitrary, superficial, ungrounded ways. What would happen if we spent as much time reflecting— wondering about and working on the inside, nurturing the things that make us who we are?

Understanding what matters most to us and discovering who we might become, and then help as a result, is the real work of our lives. Understanding how our strengths and our stories change how others see themselves is the work we're all here to do.

One of the things we do when we try to make sense of life-altering or world-changing events is to place ourselves back in that moment in time. You will often here people speak about where they were when the awful events of September 11th happened, or of the feeling they experienced when they saw Nelson Mandela walk free and Barack Obama take the oath of office. When we witness humanity, hope or truth prevail, we somehow know that these are the moments that make us.

I remember where I was on an ordinary English Saturday in May eighteen years ago. It was the day before my middle son's fifth birthday and I was shopping for birthday candles and balloons, while my husband looked after our boys at home. I was also on a mission to buy something for my brother who lived in Dublin, four hundred kilometres away, as the crow flies, across the Irish sea. I was looking for a picture frame for the black-and-white photo I'd found in an old album. My brother John was about two years old in the photo. He was wearing a white collared shirt under a spotless jumper, a pair of freshly pressed shorts and a triumphant smile. His hair was a thick shock of white, bleached by too few sunny Irish summer days. You couldn't see the particular blue of his eyes, but their light was magnificent. He was leaning against a cherry blossom tree, with what looked like a wrench from my uncle's toolbox in his hand—probably given to him as a result of some irrational toddler demand, to make him stand still for the photo. The big tree and the landscape around him were dwarfed by his presence. His personality filled the frame.

I planned to send him the framed photo by express post on Monday. I remember standing in the aisle of the shop, thinking about how he would feel when he opened it the following week. I didn't know he was probably taking his last breath at that moment. By the time I got home with the candles and balloons, he was gone. My husband took the call while I was out. 'Johnny didn't make it,' he said.

My brother had been in hospital since December the previous year. He'd only spent half a day out of the place in five months. The chemotherapy had taken its toll. He no longer looked like himself. He was older and frailer than a thirty-one-year-old had a right to be. Hardly recognisable. He had long ago stopped passing a hand over his shiny scalp as he looked for himself in the mirror. Every ounce of his strength was saved for fighting—for himself, his wife, his two little girls and the things he hadn't yet had a chance to do. His eyes, though, were still that magnificent blue.

My irrational hope was that the old black-and-white photo would sit on his hospital locker and remind him of who he was. I wanted that little guy standing next to a tree in an ordinary suburban garden to look him in the eye and show him: *This* is who you are. *You* are worth fighting for.

It's hard to say exactly how witnessing the death of someone close to you changes the way you live your life. But if seemingly irrelevant events or even chance encounters can alter the direction of our lives, then it stands to reason, and beyond reason too, that the most painful and joyful experiences in our lives can also change their direction. I know this has been true for me.

My life's trajectory was changed by watching my brother die—by knowing that he would never meet the incredible women his daughters would become, and realising that he'd never get the chance to see the buildings he wanted to design be built. His death is part of my backstory and my future story too. I carry him with me in my heart and in my work today. My job involves doing for others what I couldn't do for Johnny—holding up a mirror at just the right angle, so that remarkable people and organisations, who have the power to change the world, see themselves more clearly, so they can realise their potential and do work they're proud of. We don't have a second to waste.

CREATING THE FUTURE WE WANT TO SEE

'Life can only be understood backwards; but it must be lived forwards.'
— *Søren Kierkegaard*

In April 2014, Oliver Schmidt, general manager of Volkswagen's environment and engineering in the United States, was informed that independent testing at West Virginia University found that emissions from VW diesel cars vastly exceeded federal standards. Later that same day, he emailed a colleague to raise the alarm. 'It should first be decided whether we are honest. If we are not honest, everything stays as it is,' he wrote.

As 2016 was drawing to a close, FBI Special Agent Ian Dinsmore signed and filed an affidavit in support of a criminal complaint establishing probable cause for the arrest of Oliver Schmidt. Schmidt's alleged crime was knowingly participating in a conspiracy, spanning more than nine years, to defraud both Volkswagen customers and the United States government by impeding the lawful functions of the Environmental Protection Agency. A month later, Schmidt was arrested while trying to return to Germany after a family holiday in Florida. He stood trial in the summer of 2017.

At the end of November—a week before Schmidt was due to be sentenced—Volkswagen's new CEO, Matthias Müller, took the stage in Wolfsburg to speak to the company's workforce. He expressed his frustration about the pace of progress towards culture change in the company. 'In many places, we are still too slow, too bureaucratic and too hierarchical.' But '2017 was a good year for Volkswagen Group,' he said, thanking his team of 630,000 colleagues around the world. Buoyed by strong demand in China and Europe, the Volkswagen Group was on track to achieve a record year of sales. The company had achieved its goal of being number one. 'Despite the diesel crisis, we have kept our sights firmly fixed on the future—not just with a view to tomorrow's focus areas, but also with regard to the vehicles and technologies with which we earn our money today and will continue doing so for many years to come.' Volkswagen was back.

Before he was sentenced on 6th December 2017 in Detroit, Oliver Schmidt—the man who had become the face of the Volkswagen emissions scandal, who felt 'misused' by his former employer—read a letter to the court accepting both blame and his fate. He wished he had 'done things differently', but said he knew that 'none of that was of any use' now. 'I'm deeply sorry for the wrongs I've committed, and I'm as ready as I'll ever be to accept my punishment now.'

U.S. District Judge Sean Cox addressed the accused. 'I'm sure, based on common sense, that you viewed this cover-up as your opportunity to shine. That your goal was to impress senior management to fix this problem—to make yourself look better, to increase your opportunities to climb the corporate ladder at VW.' Cox told the courtroom that 'This crime ... attacks and destroys the very foundation of our economic system: That is trust.' He then sentenced Schmidt to seven years in prison and fined him $400,000.

You might be left with the impression that in the scheme of things, Volkswagen got off lightly. It seems like they simply have to go through the legal channels, pay the fines owed and fix the affected vehicles, and everything will right itself. They're still in business and delivering good returns for shareholders. Doesn't that mean they're successful? I'd argue that profits alone are not what makes a successful company. A great company respects and nurtures the people it employs and the customers it serves. A great company doesn't just thrive because it's profitable; it's profitable because it helps people to thrive. Great companies leave the world better than they found it—which is why those of us responsible for creating and building businesses must be as clear about the way we get to our destination as we are about what that destination is.

We often talk about finding our way as we navigate through life. I'd argue that we're creating our way instead, by understanding what success means to us and being deliberate and intentional about working towards it. You might remember when you were a high school student (as I do), trying to create a study system to help you maximise your chances of academic success. Teachers held up model students as examples of how hard work paid off. Straight-A students, it seemed, were just the ones who did 'the most' work. And 'most', being infinite, was a daunting place to start.

It's taken me a good thirty years to realise that exceptional performance is not a result of expending the most effort— trying to get to the summit in a single, spectacular leap. Or reaching some arbitrary destination along a route that others have determined as the right one. The secret to being exceptional is in the small choices we make moment-to-moment. The student who organises his notes from the very first lecture of the first semester. The tram driver who makes his passengers smile on a wet Monday morning. The airline lounge attendant who cares. The athlete who pushes through the last three uncomfortable repetitions. The CEO who intentionally seeks out and acts on the wisdom of her team. The doctor who greets his patients warmly, shaking them by the hand. Ordinary people, making small choices that transform them into the people who are creating the future we all want to see.

We can sometimes compromise as we navigate the path to success. But if we 'make it' by doing things that don't resonate with our values or by forsaking our humanity and identity, we will never feel like a success. We meet success and fulfilment in our eyes the day we can look in the mirror and say, hand on heart, 'today I did something I'm proud to have done'. Each of us has a choice. We get to choose what to care about and create. We're the ones who decide what to prioritise today and what it's important to strive for tomorrow. We can decide whether to compete or to matter. And even when we don't get to choose the work, how we do it is always a choice.

Physician and author Atul Gawande talks about how making the choice to ask a simple question changed both his practice and outcomes for his patients, many of whom face terminal illness or a life-limiting diagnosis. He wanted to change the conversation about patient care that revolved around choosing either to fight the disease or to give up. He began by asking patients what a good day looked like for them. This very act meant that the more important questions about what he and his patients were fighting for were answered. The patients' priorities and reasons to be alive could then be acknowledged and attended to by the medical team. Gawande's question is relevant in guiding both our personal and professional decisions, even when death is not imminent. The only way to avoid sacrificing what's truly important in the face of external pressures is to understand the 'what fors' and why they matter.

What does your good day look like? What are your reasons to be alive and doing what you do as only you can? You need to know. Because what we do today affects who we'll become tomorrow. We have to make sure we don't forgo asking the important questions along the way. And more, we must do everything we can to deliberately create the good days that are the making of us. Our collective prosperity depends on motivated individuals who know how they can contribute. When we are true to ourselves, everything changes. We owe it to ourselves and to our children to show them how it's done. It will be the making of us all.

RESOURCES

To download the free PDF of
the Story-Driven Framework and for more
information about business storytelling
workshops, please visit:
thestoryoftelling.com/books/story-driven

REFERENCES

PREFACE

'To know who you are' — Sherrilyn Kenyon and Dianna Love, *Blood Trinity: Belador Book 1* (New York: Simon and Schuster, 2010)

We Are More Powerful Than We Think

'The most powerful person in the world' — Steve Jobs, 1994 conversation quoted by Tomas Higbey in a post on Quora, 1 July 2013. https://www.quora.com/Steve-Jobs/What-are-the-best-stories-about-people-randomly-or-non-randomly-meeting-Steve-Jobs/answer/Tomas-Higbey

Qantas employs 30,000 people — 'Our Company', Qantas.com. https://www.qantas.com/travel/airlines/company/global/en

INTRODUCTION

'[S]uccess is like a mountain' — George Saunders, convocation speech, University of Syracuse, New York, 11 May 2013. Reproduced in full at *The New York Times 6ᵗʰ Floor Blog*: https://6thfloor.blogs.nytimes.com/2013/07/31/george-saunderss-advice-to-graduates/

'Millions of people across the world…' — Mark Thompson and Ivana Kottasova, 'Volkswagen scandal widens', CNN Money, 22 September 2015. http://money.cnn.com/2015/09/22/news/vw-recall-diesel/index.html

'[W]e had some targets' — Matthias Mueller, Volkswagen CEO, National Public Radio interview, 11 January 2016. http://www.npr.org/sections/thetwo-way/2016/01/11/462682378/we-didnt-lie-volkswagen-ceo-says-of-emissions-scandal

Consumer Reports ranked Tesla — Benjamin Zhang, '*Consumer Reports* names Tesla the top American car brand', *Business Insider Australia,* 1 March 2017. https://www.businessinsider.com.au/consumer-reports-tesla-top-america-car-brand-2017-2?r=US&IR=

The company produces more vehicles in two days — Eric Loveday, 'Volkswagen Says It Can "Stop" Tesla With Its "Abilities Tesla Doesn't Have"', *Inside EVs,* 8 July 2017. http://insideevs.com/volkswagen-says-edge-tesla-electric-car-segment/

'The group's strategy' and further quotations — Volkswagen AG Annual Report 2011, 'Strategy 2018': http://annualreport2011.volkswagenag.com/managementreport/reportonexpecteddevelopments/strategy/strategy2018.html

'We see Volkswagen as the company' — Christoph Rauwald, 'Late to the Battery Car Race, VW Says It Can Still Blunt Tesla', *Bloomberg Business Week,* 6 July 2017. https://www.bloomberg.com/news/articles/2017-07-07/late-to-the-battery-car-race-vw-says-it-can-still-blunt-tesla

'Anything Tesla can do' — Patrick McGee, 'Volkswagen plans to "leapfrog" Tesla in electric car race', *Financial Times,* 7 May 2017. https://www.ft.com/content/a43ac2ce-3198-11e7-9555-23ef563ecf9a

'[T]o accelerate the world's transition' — 'About Tesla', Tesla.com, retrieved 25 January 2018. https://www.tesla.com/about

'As you know' — Elon Musk, 'The Secret Tesla Motors Master Plan (just between you and me)', Tesla Motors blog, Tesla.com, 2 August 2006. https://www.tesla.com/en_AU/blog/secret-tesla-motors-master-plan-just-between-you-and-me

Prior to the emissions scandal — Leah McGrath Goodman, 'Why Volkswagen Cheated', *Newsweek*, 15 December 2015. http://www.newsweek.com/2015/12/25/why-volkswagen-cheated-404891.html

The Downside of Playing to Win

'Since finite games are played to be won' —James P. Carse, *Finite and Infinite Games: A Vision of Life as Play and Possibility.* (New York: Free Press, 1986)

Redefining Greatness

Uber's valuation of $70 billion early in 2017 — https://equidateinc.com/company/uber

The string of scandals — Biz Carson and Skye Gould, 'Uber's bad year: The stunning string of blows that upended the world's most valuable startup', *Business Insider,* 26 June, 2017. http://www.businessinsider.com/uber-scandal-crisis-complete-timeline-2017-6?IR=T

'[W]inning gave some excuses' — Cale Guthrie Weissman, 'Dara Khosrowshahi says Uber was winning too much to fix its broken culture', FastCompany.com, 9 November 2017. https://www.fastcompany.com/40494063/dara-khosrowshahi-says-uber-was-winning-too-much-to-fix-its-broken-culture

PART ONE

'The critical question is not "How can I achieve?"' — Peter F. Drucker, *The Daily Drucker: 366 Days of Insight and Motivation for Getting the Right Things Done,* foreword by Jim Collins. (New York: HarperBusiness, 2004)

The Reason

Belief in the significance of what we're doing — Viktor Frankl, *Man's Search For Meaning.* (Boston: Beacon Press, 2006)

In one study — David S. Yeager, Marlone Henderson, et al., 'Boring but Important: A Self-Transcendent Purpose for Learning Academic Self-Regulation', *Journal of Personality and Social Psychology,* Vol. 107 No. 4. https://web.stanford. edu/~paunesku/articles/yeager_2014.pdf

Meaning Is a Competitive Advantage

[M]eaning's 'essential quality' — Dan Ariely, *Payoff: The Hidden Logic That Shapes Our Motivations.* (New York: Simon & Schuster, 2016)

'An experiment is under way' — Robert Safian, 'Facebook, Airbnb, Uber, and the Struggle to Do the Right Thing', *Fast Company,* 11 April 2017. https://www.fastcompany. com/40397294/facebook-airbnb-uber-and-the-struggle-to-do-the-right-thing

Narrative and Identity

Story is defined — Definition from http://www.dictionary.com/ browse/story

How our personality develops over time — Dan P. McAdams, Kate C. McLean. 'Narrative Identity', *Current Directions in Psychological Science.* Vol. 22 No. 3. http://journals.sagepub.com/ doi/abs/10.1177/0963721413475622

'In personality psychology' — Dan P. McAdams, *The Art and Science of Personality Development*. (New York: The Guilford Press, 2015)

Background information about autobiographical memory —

— Martin A. Conway and Christopher W. Pleydell-Pearce, 'The Construction of Autobiographical Memories in the Self-Memory System', *Psychological Review*, 2000, Vol. 107, No. 2. http://citeseerx.ist.psu.edu/viewdoc/download?doi=10.1.1.621.9717&rep=rep1&type=pdf

— Dorthe Berntsen and David C. Rubin, editors, *Understanding Autobiographical Memory: Theories and Approaches*. (Cambridge: Cambridge University Press, 2012)

Who Do You Think You Are?

'[C]ompanies are increasingly seeking' — Robert Safian, 'Facebook, Airbnb, Uber, and the Struggle to Do the Right Thing', Fast Company, 11 April 2017. https://www.fastcompany.com/40397294/facebook-airbnb-uber-and-the-struggle-to-do-the-right-thing

'Create stunning solar roofs' — Steve Hanley, 'Elon Musk reveals Tesla Master Plan Part 2: Solar, Pickup and Ride Share', Teslarati.com, 20 July 2016. https://www.teslarati.com/elon-musk-reveals-tesla-master-plan-part-2-solar-pickup-ride-share/

The Narrative Effect

Reciprocity bias — Crawford Hollingworth, 'Bias In the Spotlight: Reciprocity', ResearchLive.com, 28 July 2015. https://www.research-live.com/article/opinion/bias-in-the-spotlight-reciprocity/id/4013678

Conformity bias — Saul McLeod, 'Asch Experiment', SimplyPsychology.com, 2008. https://www.simplypsychology. org/asch-conformity.html

The brain can also adapt — Carol Dweck, *Mindset: The New Psychology of Success.* (New York: Random House, 2006)

'"You will know"—The Real Leadership Lessons of Steve Jobs', Walter Isaacson, *Harvard Business Review*, April 2012. https:// hbr.org/2012/04/the-real-leadership-lessons-of-steve-jobs

Everlane's culture centres around radical transparency — Everlane.com, https://www.everlane.com/about

The Business of Story

Worldwide ad spending — 'Worldwide Ad Spending: The eMarketer Forecast for 2017', eMarketer.com, 12 April 2017. https://www.emarketer.com/Report/Worldwide-Ad-Spending-eMarketer-Forecast-2017/2002019

'[S]ilent trade' — 'Silent trade', *Encyclopaedia Britannica.* https:// global.britannica.com/topic/silent-trade

'[M]ore important to have a strong corporate purpose' — '20th CEO Survey: 20 years inside the mind of the CEO... What's next?' PwC. https://www.pwc.com/gx/en/ceo-survey/2017/pwc-ceo-20th-survey-report-2017.pdf

'[F]or-profit companies' and further quotations — 'What are B Corps?', Bcorporation.net, https://www.bcorporation.net/what-are-b-corps

Story As Strategy

'[M]ake it easy to do business anywhere' and further quotations — 'Company Overview', Alibabagroup.com, http://www. alibabagroup.com/en/about/overview

'We know well we haven't survived because' — Jillian D'Onfro, 'How Jack Ma Went From Being A Poor School Teacher To Turning Alibaba Into A $US160 Billion Behemoth', *Business Insider Australia*, 15 September 2014. https://www. businessinsider.com.au/the-story-of-jack-ma-founder-of-alibaba-2014-9?r=US&IR=T

'[W]hile shareholders expect us to be profitable — '2017 Letter to Shareholders from Executive Chairman Jack Ma', Alizila. com, 17 October 2017. http://www.alizila.com/2017-letter-shareholders-executive-chairman-jack-ma/

The Story-Driven Framework

[W]e overestimate how motivated people are by money — Dan Ariely, Emir Kamenica, and Drazen Pelec, 'Man's Search for Meaning: The Case of Legos', *Journal of Economic Behavior and Organization,* Volume 67, Issues 3–4, September 2008, Pages 671-677.

Backstory — 'How Jack Ma Went From Being A Poor School Teacher To Turning Alibaba Into A $US160 Billion Behemoth', Jillian D'Onfro, *Business Insider Australia*, 15 September 2014. https://www.businessinsider.com.au/the-story-of-jack-ma-founder-of-alibaba-2014-9?r=US&IR=T

Values — 'Culture and Values', Alibabagroup.com, http://www. alibabagroup.com/en/about/culture

Purpose and Vision — 'Company Overview', Alibabagroup.com, http://www.alibabagroup.com/en/about/overview

Strategy —

— Joe Mcdonald, 'Here's the Story of Alibaba's Rise', *Business Insider,* 9 May 2014. http://www.businessinsider. com/here-is-the-story-of-alibabas-rise-2014-5?IR=T

— 'History and Milestones', Alibabagroup.com, http://
www.alibabagroup.com/en/about/history

— Piet Walraven, 'A Brief History (and Future) of Alibaba.
com', Technode.com, 22 January 2009. http://technode.
com/2009/01/22/a-brief-history-and-future-of-alibabacom/

PART TWO

'Business isn't always about numbers' — Robert Safian, 'Trust
Your Feelings, Now More Than Ever', *Fast Company*, 14 August
2017. https://www.fastcompany.com/40437744/trust-your-
feelings-now-more-than-ever

Building a Story-Driven Company

'We're absent from this community' — Jordan Lebeau, 'Starbucks
Hopes 15 New Stores Will Make It Part Of The 'DNA' Of
Low-Income Communities Of Color', *Forbes*, 13 October
2016. https://www.forbes.com/sites/jordanlebeau/2016/10/13/
starbucks-hopes-15-new-stores-will-make-it-part-of-the-dna-
of-low-income-communities-of-color/#323aeaee4adc

'[O]ne of 15' — Karen Valbey, 'Starbucks Is Bringing Hope—and
Profit—to the Communities America's Forgotten', *Fast Company*,
31 July 2017. https://www.fastcompany.com/40438365/
starbucks-is-bringing-hope-and-profit-to-the-communities-
americas-forgotten

'We are committed to providing' — 'Our United Customer
Commitment', United.com. https://www.united.com/web/en-
US/content/customerfirst.aspx

'This is an upsetting event' — 'Response to United Express
Flight 3411', April 10, 2017. http://newsroom.united.com/news-
releases?item=124753

Maximum Impact

One by one they visited hosts — Morgan Brown, 'Airbnb: The Growth Story You Didn't Know', Growthhackers.com, 2014. https://growthhackers.com/growth-studies/airbnb

'[T]ake the pulse' — 'Airbnb Founder Brian Chesky Homeless for Almost Three Years', *Opposing Views*, 11 March 2013. https://www.opposingviews.com/i/technology/airbnb-founder-brian-chesky-homeless-almost-three-years

The Power of Your Backstory

'If you do not know' — Terry Pratchett, *I Shall Wear Midnight*. (New York: HarperCollins, 2010)

The part of the Nike origin story — Eric Ransdell, 'The Nike Story? Just Tell It!', *Fast Company*, 31 December 1999. https://www.fastcompany.com/38979/nike-story-just-tell-it

'Build the best product' — 'Patagonia's Mission Statement', Patagonia.com. http://www.patagonia.com/company-info.html

'Because Patagonia wants to be in business' — 'Don't Buy This Jacket, Black Friday, and the *New York Times*', Patagonia.com, 25 November 2011. https://www.patagonia.com/blog/2011/11/dont-buy-this-jacket-black-friday-and-the-new-york-times

'Health insurance was the first thing we did' — Emily Canal, 'Why Howard Schultz Says Good Leaders Always Have a Social Purpose—No Matter What the Companies Sell', *Inc.*, 28 September 2017. https://www.inc.com/emily-canal/howard-schultz-on-why-the-best-leaders-have-social-purpose.html

The Importance of Values

Zappos core values — 'Zappos 10 Core Values', Zapposinsights.com. https://www.zapposinsights.com/about/core-values

Call centre employees don't have sales scripts — 'Employee Shatters Record with 10-Hour Call', *Beyond the Box,* 4 April 2017. https://www.zappos.com/beyondthebox/record-call

The Value of Purpose

'People work better' — Elon Musk, quoted by Anthony Galli, 'Elon Musk Life Purpose Explained', Medium.com, 10 October 2017. https://medium.com/the-mission/elon-musk-life-purpose-explained-d08e7f37ce28

[W]e often do things for their own sake — Gianluca Baldassarre et al., 'Intrinsic motivations and open-ended development in animals, humans, and robots: An overview', *Frontiers In Psychology,* 9 September 2014.

The Theory of Self-Determination — 'Self-determination theory', Wikipedia. https://en.wikipedia.org/wiki/Self-determination_theory

Research by Gallup — Susan Sorenson and Keri Garmen, 'How to Tackle US Employees' Stagnating Engagement', *Gallup News,* 11 June 2013. http://www.gallup.com/businessjournal/162953/tackle-employees-stagnating-engagement.aspx

87 percent of millennials — 'Infographics: Psychology of Successfully Marketing to Millennials', University of Southern California. http://appliedpsychologydegree.usc.edu/resources/infographics/psychology-of-successfully-marketing-to-millennials/

'The authors draw on a treasure trove' — Janet Albrechtsen, 'Clinton worked the maths but Trump won the mood', *The Australian,* 3 May 2017. http://www.theaustralian.com.au/opinion/columnists/janet-albrechtsen/clinton-worked-the-maths-but-trump-won-the-mood/

'In politics, the personal narrative is vital' — Hillary Clinton, *What Happened*. (New York: Simon & Schuster, 2017)

Vision

'To begin with the end in mind' — Stephen R. Covey, *The 7 Habits of Highly Effective People*. (New York: Simon & Schuster, 2004)

'[B]uild the ecosystem for work' — 'Making work simpler, more pleasant, and more productive', Slack.com. https://slack.com/about

'[I]f we are selling "a reduction in the cost of communication"' — Stewart Butterfield, 'We Don't Sell Saddles Here', Medium.com, 17 February 2014. https://medium.com/@stewart/we-dont-sell-saddles-here-4c59524d650d

At the time of this writing — Chris Von Wilpert, 'Peek Inside Slack's Multi-Million Dollar SAAS Growth Strategy', *Openview*, 12 July 2017. https://labs.openviewpartners.com/slack-saas-growth-strategy/#.WgkD5oZxVAY

Seventy-seven percent of the Fortune 500 — '52 Amazing Slack Statistics and Facts', *DMR*, December 2017. https://expandedramblings.com/index.php/slack-statistics/

The company has gone from zero — Matthew Lynley, 'Slack raises a huge financing round from SoftBank valuing the company at $5.1B', TechCrunch.com, 17 September 2017. https://techcrunch.com/2017/09/17/slack-raises-a-huge-financing-round-from-softbank-valuing-the-company-at-5-1b/

Strategy

'If you don't know where you're going' — George Harrison, 'Any Road'. (Parlophone Records, 2003)

Likewise, when Jack Ma envisaged — 'Alibaba: From Start to Now (and Wow)', PYMNTS.com, 18 September 2014. https://www.pymnts.com/news/2014/alibaba-from-start-to-now-and-wow/

'Build sports car' — Elon Musk, 'The Secret Tesla Motors Master Plan (just between you and me)', Tesla Motors blog, Tesla.com, 2 August 2006. https://www.tesla.com/en_AU/blog/secret-tesla-motors-master-plan-just-between-you-and-me

Case Stories

'A business that makes nothing but money' — Henry Ford, 'Mr. Ford's Own Page', *New York Tribune*, 19 January 1919, as shown on the following Library of Congress webpage: https://chroniclingamerica.loc.gov/lccn/sn83030214/1919-01-19/ed-1/seq-41/#date1=1836&index=0&rows=20&searchType=advanced&language=&sequence=0&words=business+kind+money+poor&proxdistance=5&date2=1922&ortext=&proxtext=&phrasetext=money+is+a+poor+kind+of+business&andtext=&dateFilterType=yearRange&page=1

Tesla Motors

Elon Musk was born and raised — Elon Musk Viral Videos, 'Elon Musk talks about his Crazy Grandfather', 17 August 2017. https://www.youtube.com/watch?v=r5-jyn59IzU

Elon Musk inherited a lifetime of adventure — Mark Melnychuk, *Regina Leader-Post,* 12 May 2017. http://leaderpost.com/feature/elon-musk-inherited-a-lifetime-of-adventure-from-his-sask-family

The young Elon Musk — 'Blastar 1984 (web version).' https://blastar-1984.appspot.com/

As a teenager, Musk was influenced —

— Ashlee Vance, Elon Musk: Tesla, SpaceX and the Quest for a Fantastic Future. (New York: Ecco Press, 2015)

— '"Elon Musk," a Biography by Ashlee Vance, Paints a Driven Portrait', Dwight Garner, *New York Times*, 12 May 2015. https://www.nytimes.com/2015/05/13/books/elon-musk-a-biography-by-ashlee-vance-paints-a-driven-portrait.html

Purpose, Vision, and Strategy —

— Elon Musk, 'The Secret Tesla Motors Master Plan (just between you and me)', Tesla Motors blog, Tesla.com, 2 August 2006. <https://www.tesla.com/en_AU/blog/secret-tesla-motors-master-plan-just-between-you-and-me>

— Elon Musk, 'Master Plan Part Deux', Tesla.com, 20 July 2016. https://www.tesla.com/blog/master-plan-part-deux

Tesla was *Consumer Reports'* top-ranked car brand — Benjamin Zhang, 'Consumer Reports names Tesla the top American car brand', *Business Insider Australia*, 1 March 2017. https://www.businessinsider.com.au/consumer-reports-tesla-top-america-car-brand-2017-2?r=US&IR=T

Additional background information —

— 'Total CO_2 Saved by Tesla Vehicle Owners', Tesla.com, December 2017. https://www.tesla.com/en_AU/carbonimpact

— Jeff Dunn, 'Tesla is valued as high as Ford and GM — but that has nothing to do with what it's done so far', *Business Insider Australia*, 12 April 2017. https://www.businessinsider.com.au/tesla-value-vs-ford-gm-chart-2017-4?r=US&IR=T

— Johana Buiyan, 'Tesla saw about 63,000 cancellations of Model 3 preorders', Recode, 2 August 2017. https://www.recode.net/2017/8/2/16087432/tesla-model-3-electric-car-manufacture-preorder-cancellations-elon-musk

— Alex Davies, 'Meet the Tesla Semitruck, Elon Musk's Most Electrifying Gamble Yet', *Wired*, 16 November 2017. https://www.wired.com/story/tesla-truck-revealed/

Emma Bridgewater Pottery

Background information —

— Ted Institute, 'Emma Bridgewater: How an entrepreneurial potter helped restore beauty to a city', 4 September, 2015. https://www.youtube.com/watch?v=-MHwNI9bJj0

— 'Emma Bridgewater', *Wikipedia*. https://en.wikipedia.org/wiki/Emma_Bridgewater

Strategy — 'Emma Bridgewater teams with Liberty', Licensingsource.net, 15 September, 2016. http://www.licensingsource.net/emma-bridgwater-teams-with-liberty

In 2016 Emma Bridgewater's annual revenue and other background information —

— 'Pottery firm Emma Bridgewater creates 70 jobs in £1m investment', BBC.com, 20 September 2016. http://www.bbc.com/news/uk-england-stoke-staffordshire-37410643

— 'Emma Bridgewater', *Birmingham Made Me*, http://birmingham-made-me.org/emma-bridgewater-case-study/#.WffNGIZxVAY

— Anna Tyzack, 'Pottery queen Emma Bridgewater: "Unhappiness is a great driver"', *Telegraph,* 17 March 2014. http://www.telegraph.co.uk/women/womens-business/10694631/Emma-Bridgewater-Unhappiness-is-a-great-driver.html

— 'About Us', EmmaBridgewater.co.uk, http://www.emmabridgewater.co.uk/en/uk/pcat/aboutus

'You're thinking about a ten-year horizon' — 'Emma Bridgewater', BBC Radio 4, 2 December 2016. http://www.bbc.co.uk/programmes/b083m2zq

Miss Gertrude Salon

Background information —

— 'Miss Gertrude', MyLocalSalon.com, http://www.mylocalsalon.com.au/missgertrude.html

— 'History', MissGertrude.com, https://www.missgertrude.com/history

— Leanne Spence, personal interviews, October 2017 and January 2018.

Wikipedia

Background information —

— 'Jimmy Wales', Wikipedia, https://en.wikipedia.org/wiki/Jimmy_Wales

— 'History of Wikipedia', *Wikipedia*, https://en.wikipedia.org/wiki/History_of_Wikipedia

— 'Wikipedia', Wikipedia, https://en.wikipedia.org/wiki/Wikipedia

Purpose — 'Wikipedia: Five pillars', Wikipedia, https://simple.wikipedia.org/wiki/Wikipedia:Five_pillars

Les Mills Group

Les Mills choreographed his first barbell workout — 'The Les Mills Story', LesMills.com, https://www.lesmills.com/about-us/our-story/

'Transform the global health system' — 'Les Mills Values', https://www.slideshare.net/stevenrenata/les-mills-values

Same Day Dental

Background information — Dr. Charles Cole, personal interview, January 2018.

Finland's Baby Welcome Kits

Background information —

— 'History of the Maternity Grant', Kela.fi, http://www.kela.fi/web/en/maternity-grant-history

— 'Maternity Package', *Wikipedia,* https://en.wikipedia.org/wiki/Maternity_package

— Eli Rosenberg, 'Why Finland's Newborns Sleep in Cardboard Cribs' —*New York Times*, 6 July 2016. https://www.nytimes.com/2016/07/07/world/what-in-the-world/finland-baby-box.html

— Rachael Pells, '"Every Child Is Equal": How Finland's Baby Boxes Changed Childhood', *Independent*, 14 October 2016. http://www.independent.co.uk/life-style/health-and-families/finland-baby-box-moomin-childcare-scandinavia-welfare-a7356916.html

— Stacey Macintosh and Jhannine Verceles, 'The Future of the Finnish Baby Box', MS thesis, Laurea University of Applied Sciences, May 2017. https://www.theseus.fi/bitstream/handle/10024/125636/Thesis_Stacey%20and%20Jhannine_31032017.pdf?sequence=1

— Hanna Markkula-Kivisilta, 'How Finland Puts Moms First', *Huffington Post*, 8 July 2013. https://www.huffingtonpost.com/hanna-markkulakivisilta/jnj-finland-mothers-health_b_3534146.html

— 'Maternal Health', SaveTheChildren.org, http://www.savethechildren.org/site/c.8rKLIXMGIpI4E/b.9391183/k.9B53/Mothers_Day.htm?msource=wenlpmod0516

James Day Wedding Photography

Background information — James Day, personal interview, November 2017.

The Virgin Group

Background information —

— 'About us', Virgin.com, https://www.virgin.com/virgingroup/content/about-us

— 'Richard Branson on Crafting Your Mission Statement', Richard Branson, Facebook.com, https://www.facebook.com/notes/fodson-foday-kamara/richard-branson-on-crafting-your-mission-statement/629953063689283/

— 'Our story', VirginAtlantic.com, https://www.virginatlantic.com/gb/en/footer/our-story.html

— 'Why did Richard Branson start an airline?', Virgin.com, https://www.virgin.com/travel/why-did-richard-branson-start-airline

Vision — 'The End of Business As Usual', TheBTeam.com, http://bteam.org/planb/#drive-full-transparency

The Michelin Group

Andre and Edouard Michelin were seventeen and eleven —

— 'Our purpose', Michelin.com. https://www.michelin.com/eng/michelin-group/profile/our-purpose

— 'Michelin', *Wikipedia,* https://en.wikipedia.org/wiki/Michelin

Values and Purpose —The Michelin Brand: Trust and Progress', Michelin.com, https://www.michelin.com/eng/media-room/press-and-news/michelin-news/Passion/The-Michelin-brand-trust-and-progress

'Imagine a future' — 'Michelin Visionary Concept', Michelin.com, https://www.michelin.com/eng/media-room/press-and-news/michelin-news/Innovation/MICHELIN-Visionary-Concept

Strategy — 'Us Tomorrow', Michelin.com, https://www.michelin.com/eng/michelin-group/strategy/Us-tomorrow

IKEA

Background information —

— 'IKEA history – how it all began', IKEA.com, http://www.ikea.com/ms/en_AU/about_ikea/the_ikea_way/history/

— 'Ingvar Kamprad, founder of IKEA', Sweden.se, https://sweden.se/business/ingvar-kamprad-founder-of-ikea/

— Oliver Burkeman, 'The Miracle of Älmhult', *Guardian*, 17 June 2004. https://www.theguardian.com/lifeandstyle/2004/jun/17/shopping.retail https://en.wikipedia.org/wiki/IKEA

— 'The Testament of a Furniture Dealer', IKEA.com, http://www.ikea.com/ms/en_AU/pdf/reports-downloads/the-testament-of-a-furniture-dealer.pdf

— Noah Friedman, 'Here's the meaning behind all of those obscure IKEA product names', *Business Insider Australia*, 21 October 2017. https://www.businessinsider.com.au/ikea-product-naming-system-meaning-2017-10?r=US&IR=T

Purpose — About the IKEA Group, http://www.ikea.com/ms/en_US/this-is-ikea/company-information/index.html

Values — Craig Pratt, 'A Dose of Swedishness', Ikea.com, https://highlights.ikea.com/2017/a-dose-of-swedishness/

Strategy —

— 'People & Planet Positive: IKEA Group Sustainability Strategy for 2020', IKEA.com, http://www.ikea.com/ms/en_CA/pdf/reports-downloads/sustainability-strategy-people-and-planet-positive.pdf

— 'The IKEA Concept', http://www.ikea.com/ms/en_AU/this-is-ikea/the-ikea-concept/index.html

Heat Holders Thermal Socks

When Heat Holders launched in 2008 — 'Our Story', Heatholders.com, https://www.heatholders.com/pages/our-story

Background information — Shane Doughty, personal interview, September 2017.

Small Giants

'Compared to the massiveness' — Big Hearted Business, 'BHB Inspiration Bomb – Berry Liberman Part 1', 1 August 2013. https://www.youtube.com/watch?time_continue=871&v=cl9hlsjaePk

Berry was on a mission of her own — Mikki Brammer, 'Berry Liberman', *Map Magazine Weekend Edition.* http://theweekendedition.com.au/mapmagazine/berry-liberman/

Values — 'Philosophy', Smallgiants.com, http://www.smallgiants.com.au/our-philosophy/

Strategy — 'Portfolio', Smallgiants.com, http://www.smallgiants.com.au/sgcapital/

Melbourne's Happiest Tram Driver

It's hard to imagine —

— Jill Stark, 'Melbourne's happiest tram driver brings joy and connection to the daily grind', *The Age,* 24 January 2016. http://www.theage.com.au/victoria/melbournes-happiest-tram-driver-brings-joy-and-connection-to-the-daily-grind-20160123-gmclcl.html

— 'Tram driver's fantastic Christmas customer service', *7 News Australia,* 25 December 2015. https://www.facebook.com/7NewsAustralia/posts/1189854771024714

Background information — Bruce Whalley, personal interview, November 2017.

Fiasco Gelato

'Yes, we started by making' — 'James Boetcher On How He Built the Fiasco Gelato Brand', *A Branded World Podcast – 006,* Luiza Campos, Marcastrategy.com. http://marcastrategy.com/podcast_files/006/ABrandedWorld_006_ShowTranscript.pdf

'We have grown almost 6000%' — 'Who We Are', Fiascogelato.ca, https://www.fiascogelato.ca/about/

Background information — James Boettcher, email interview, January 2018.

PART THREE

'The one thing that you have' — Neil Gaiman, 'Keynote Address 2012', University of the Arts Commencement, 17 May 2012. https://www.uarts.edu/neil-gaiman-keynote-address-2012

CONCLUSION

The Making of Us

'You can't connect the dots' — Steve Jobs, 'Commencement Address 2005', Stanford University, 12 June 2005. https://news.stanford.edu/2005/06/14/jobs-061505/

'I have a little shadow' — Robert Louis Stevenson, 'My Shadow', *A Child's Garden of Verses and Underwoods*. (New York: Current Literature, 1906)

One of our favourite books — Eric Carle, *The Very Hungry Caterpillar*. (Cleveland: World Publishing, 1969)

Creating the Future We Want to See

Buoyed by strong demand — Bertel Schmitt, 'It's Official: Volkswagen Is World's Largest Automaker in 2016. Or Maybe Toyota.' *Forbes*, 30 January 2017. https://www.forbes.com/sites/bertelschmitt/2017/01/30/its-official-volkswagen-worlds-largest-automaker-2016-or-maybe-toyota/4/#bed81f44dba4

'Despite the diesel crisis' — Matthias Müller, Address to Works Meeting, December 2017. https://www.volkswagen-media-services.com/en/detailpage/-/detail/Mller-and-Osterloh-We-came-a-long-way-in-2017-Now-our-job-is-to-keep-it-up/view/5922329/7a5bbec13158edd433c6630f5ac445da?p_p_auth=zMGZ0j10

'I'm deeply sorry' — Larry P. Vellequette, 'Ex-VW exec Schmidt gets max 7 years, $400,000 fine for U.S. emissions violations', *Automotive News Europe,* 6 December 2017. http://europe. autonews.com/article/20171206/COPY/312069936/ex-vw-exec-schmidt-gets-max-7-years-$400000-fine-for-u.s.-emissions

Physician and author Atul Gawande — 'What Matters in the End', *On Being,* 26 October 2017. https://onbeing.org/programs/ atul-gawande-what-matters-in-the-end-oct2017

ACKNOWLEDGEMENTS

Thank you for buying *Story Driven* and for reading this far. I don't take that for granted in our busy world full of demands on your time. It's been a privilege to write it for you, and I hope it helps you to build a career and business you can be proud of. I'd love to hear about how you're using the book to do that. You can email me at hello@thestoryoftelling.com to let me know how you're putting the ideas in the book to work.

I'm grateful for the remarkable, loyal readers of my blog, whom I get to share ideas with each week. They inspire me every day and give me a reason to write.

Thanks to the entrepreneurs and organisations whose contributions and stories shaped this book: Elon Musk, The Mills Family, Berry Liberman, Bruce Whalley, Michael Preysman, Emma Bridgewater, Howard Schultz, Leanne Spence, Jimmy Wales, Shane Doughty, Charles Cole, Mark Dyck, Jack Ma, James Boettcher, James Day, Ingvar Kamprad, Richard Branson, Atul Gawande, Qantas, Tesla, Patagonia, ASSA ABLOY and Michelin. You are creating the future we all want to see.

Thank you to the experts, journalists and podcasters who generously share ideas with us, particularly Professor Dan

McAdams, James Carse, and the teams at *Fast Company*, The School of Life, Desert Island Discs, On Being, Hidden Brain and TED, who informed and influenced me as I wrote.

This book would not be in your hands without the care and talent of my designers, Reese Spykerman and Kelly Exeter, and my editor, Catherine Oliver, who create magic because they pour their hearts into everything they do. Thanks for helping me to bring this idea to life. Thanks to Noam Shahaf, who can spot a typo at fifty paces, for taking time from his already full life to proofread the manuscript, and to Néna Rawdah for her research and fact checking.

They say you are the sum of the people you surround yourself with—I know that to be true. Thanks to my friend Seth Godin for nudging, commenting and encouraging me to dig deeper as I wrote and even when I thought I was done.

Thanks to my darling husband, Moyez, and my boys, Adam, Kieran and Matthew, for being who you are. You are the best part of my story.

ABOUT THE AUTHOR

Bernadette Jiwa was born in Dublin, the storytelling capital of the world, and is now lucky enough to call Melbourne, Australia, the world's most liveable city, home.

Bernadette is a recognised global authority on business philosophy and the value of story in business, innovation and marketing. Named by Smart Company as one of the Top Business Thinkers of 2018, she is the author of several best-selling books on marketing and brand storytelling.

Her popular blog (TheStoryofTelling.com) was voted Best Australian Business Blog in 2012 and was featured three times in Smart Company's Best Australian Business Blog list, topping it in 2016. Seth Godin listed it as one of just nine business blogs he reads.

Bernadette advises, consults and speaks with entrepreneurs and business leaders, from startups to *Fortune* 500 companies, who want to do work they're proud of and create the future they want to see. Her work takes her from Melbourne to New York (and everywhere in between).

thestoryoftelling.com

CPSIA information can be obtained
at www.ICGtesting.com
Printed in the USA
LVHW091514101119
636878LV00003B/625/P